PORTRAIT OF A SEASIDE PARISH:
HOLY TRINITY SEATON CAREW

PORTRAIT OF A SEASIDE PARISH: HOLY TRINITY SEATON CAREW

Julie Cordiner

© Julie Cordiner, 2012

Published by Julie Cordiner

A CIP catalogue record for this book is available from the British Library.

ISBN 978-0-9574579-0-4

Book and cover design by Clare Brayshaw

Prepared and printed by:

York Publishing Services Ltd
64 Hallfield Road
Layerthorpe
York YO31 7ZQ

Tel: 01904 431213

Website: www.yps-publishing.co.uk

This book is dedicated to the faithful people associated with Seaton Carew, past and present, who have loved and cared for Holy Trinity Church, preserving it for future generations as a place of worship, fellowship, celebration and comfort

CONTENTS

FOREWORD

I am delighted that Mrs Julie Cordiner has followed the wonderful book released by the previous Vicar Revd. Bill Worley, which celebrated the Millennium in the year 2000 A.D.

This book contains facts, stories and information which will reward the reader with a rich insight into the multi-faceted history of our parish church. On reading it, I realised how little I had previously known about the men of the cloth who served this parish, the benefactors whose generosity has made this place of worship what it is today, and the hidden gems of art, furnishings and architecture to be discovered throughout our church.

My thanks to Julie and all who have assisted her on this project, and thank you for buying this book to aid our restoration appeal. You are now a benefactor in a fine tradition in history.

To God be the Glory in the church and in Jesus Christ Our Lord.

Revd. Captain Paul T. Allinson C.A.
Vicar 2012

PREFACE

Holy Trinity Church, Seaton Carew, was built in 1831, at a time when the village was gaining in popularity as a seaside resort in the North East of England. The original building did not have a chancel; the windows were plain leaded glass, and the altar was a table. Half of the seating was free for the poor, but better-off families paid pew rents. It was initially a chapel within Stranton parish, but in 1841 it became a Chapelry District of Seaton Carew, meaning baptisms, marriages and burials could be performed there.

Gradually the village grew, and so did the church. A chancel and a gallery were added in 1842. Our previous book, Trinity 2000, compiled by the previous vicar Bill Worley and myself as a Millennium celebration, gives an overview of the history of the church building and some notable events.

Yet the church is much more than a building. It has been a centre of the community for generations of people, who have come together in regular worship and fellowship. They have shared good times and bad, given and received support and friendship, and have learned about God's purpose and about the Christian faith not only from the vicar, but also from each other. A thriving social life has always been part of the package.

Many people comment on how lovely the interior of Holy Trinity is, giving a special feeling of warmth and welcome. This is a reflection of the previous generations who have loved and cared for the church as much as those who play a part in its life today. Some have said that there is a sense that the building is "soaked in prayer", which implies that those who enter and sit down for a while cannot help but absorb some of those prayers and offer some of their own in thanksgiving.

So I wanted this book to be a celebration of the people who have been part of Holy Trinity over the years. There are historical facts about the church, and about Seaton Carew, to set things in context. But the real gems are the stories of the people, their family history, occupations, homes, successes, tragedies, and a few surprises and mysteries. Some of the information relates to everyday life, helping us to understand what it was like to live in Seaton and take part in church and village life in days gone by. Some of it relates to memorable events and people who made their own distinctive mark on parish life.

Thank you to those who have helped me write this account of faith and life in Seaton Carew. Inevitably not everything can be included; I hope you will forgive any omissions. I have undertaken detailed research on the first 100 years or so, but for practical reasons I have had to limit the amount of material which relates to more recent times.

One theme in this book is the generosity of the villagers, some of whom were native Seatonians, and some of whom visited from afar and stayed. Many families have had a strong connection to Holy Trinity church, placing in it a memorial to their loved ones through generous donations. How many of us sit in church regularly and look at the windows, furniture and other features, yet don't realise how these came about? This book aims to help us all appreciate the past, as we look to the future.

At the time of writing we are calling on this generous spirit again, hoping to raise £150,000 through a Restoration Appeal to restore the external stonework which is badly eroded in places – an inevitable consequence of the harsh wind off the North Sea sweeping over the sandstone, and chemicals in the air. We are very grateful for a large grant received from the Heritage Lottery Fund, but we need to raise a substantial balance. By purchasing this book, you are making a direct contribution: all profits will go to the Restoration Fund, so we can preserve the church for future generations.

Julie Cordiner, September 2012

CHAPTER 1 - EARLY DAYS

Holy Trinity Church has been an important part of the seaside community of Seaton Carew in the North East of England for over 180 years. It has many interesting features, but as with many buildings, even regular visitors can sometimes fail to appreciate them. The church is a focal point not just for worship, but also for friendship, support, celebration and comfort. By exploring the history of the church and its people, we can better understand how and why it has developed into the Holy Trinity that we know and love today.

The life of the village and church are intertwined, so before looking at the introduction of the church into Seaton Carew in 1831, let us explore what the village was like in the years leading up to that time. The name comes from two separate elements: Seaton means the farm (or settlement) by the sea, and the land was once owned by the Carrowe family, with alternative spellings including Carou, Seton Carrewe and Seton Kerrowe.

In 1792 George Pearson of Durham bought part of the manor of Seaton, demolishing the Ship Inn and replacing it with the New Inn (later renamed the Seaton Hotel). At this time, Seaton Carew was already attracting visitors, with an advertisement in 1796 recording:

"There are promenades and pleasant walks, which… have a much fuller command than any other part of the coast, of these delightful land and sea prospects for which the neighbourhood of Hartlepool has ever been so much and justly admired. The beach at Seaton is 5 miles in length and of great breadth at low water, perfectly firm and smooth. In short, there is not perhaps in this island, at least in the North, a place so well calculated for enjoying all the comforts and delights resulting from sea-bathing at Seaton Carew. The bathing machines are moved with the utmost facility to any depth that may be required."

William Tate, Parish Clerk of the parish of Stranton (the nearest parish to Seaton), produced a little book in 1812 entitled "A Description of these highly noted watering places in the County of Durham, Hartlepool & Seaton Carew", which provides a good description of the village.

Tate describes a picturesque scene, with a great length of sand, and the Snook, the land to the south extending to the river Tees, covered with grass on which herds of cattle and sheep grazed. There were fine views towards the Cleveland Hills and Redcar/Coatham in one direction, and towards Hartlepool in the other.

The village at this time consisted of fifty to sixty inhabited houses, most of which were let out to visitors during the high season. There were plenty of local businesses providing excellent quality food: beef and mutton from nearby farms, fish from Hartlepool, fruit and vegetables from local gardens, and freshly baked bread morning and evening.

Tate noted that:

"the remains of this village that have hitherto resisted the encroachments of the ocean consist chiefly of a square green, inclosed on three sides with cottages and several good lodging-houses; and on the fourth side, which is the east, open to the sea; here the bank is from twelve to sixteen or eighteen feet high, and right perpendicular. The west side of this square has been rebuilt of late years, and the houses make a respectable appearance... the rest of the village consists of a single row (if we include two or three straggling dwellings that stand to the westward of it) which stretches to the southward, along the very brink of the sea beach; and the shore is here so low, that the front path is frequently laid under water in an easterly storm with high tides, and has at certain times even invaded the houses".

There was originally a fourth side to The Green, but a storm in January 1767 was said to have washed several houses away. Although the record does not state these houses were on The Green, in 1885 the oldest resident of the village told a reporter that the sea washed away a small cliff & washed over the houses & flooded them. They were then left to the ravages of the elements. A document written by William Scott Lithgo also states that there were two or three cottages on the east side which slid over the cliff, and that John Ness lived in one, and a Mr Robinson, known as Fat Jack, lived in another.

There is no doubt from Tate's little book that the villagers were very welcoming and could not do enough for the gentlemen-farmers, respectable tradesmen and their families who crowded in to Seaton in the summer season. Tate noted that

> *"The people of Seaton are remarkable for cleanliness, civility, and their great attention to bathers, which, no doubt, induces so many families to repeat their yearly visits".*

This made good business sense. Men and women alike had opportunities for employment related to the visitors' comforts – working in hotels and lodging-houses, in the hot and cold baths, managing laundry businesses, providing trips in pleasure boats, and tending to the horses that brought the visitors in their carriages. As well as bathing, walking by the sea or taking a carriage ride, visitors could play jack-bowls and quoits.

Bathing in the sea during the 19th century was quite a different experience to today. The bathing machines were wooden cabins on high wheels, with a door opening out on steps at one end. The bather undressed in private, by which time the horse had pulled the machine towards the sea, enabling them to step straight out into the sea. No mixed bathing was allowed. Although originally bathers were naked, modesty took precedence once Queen Victoria had ascended to the throne, and ladies were required to wear fairly cumbersome bathing outfits. The two main bathing machine operators at Seaton were the Lambs (blue machines) and the Weastells (white).

By 1805, two more inns had appeared, both on The Green. The King's Head Inn (later the Seaton Hall Hotel and now a care home) was built by Robert McDonald in 1803, and in 1827 it was converted into a private residence for a gentleman J W Richardson. The other inn here was the George and Dragon (now the Norton Hotel). The Seven Stars Inn was situated further south, later demolished and replaced with the Marine Hotel. There was no road linking Seaton to West Hartlepool until 1879.

Quaker families from Darlington (including the Pease and Backhouse families) were particularly fond of visiting the village, and performed various charitable works in Seaton Carew, including donating a lifeboat; in 1815 a lifeboat station was opened.

In the 1830s transport was available on the Royal Union mail coach, which travelled via Stockton, for those who could afford the fare of three-pence a mile to sit in a carriage. Others who were less well-off had to settle for a horse drawn mail cart, sitting among the parcels. Paddle steamers and other boat trips also delivered visitors to the village.

Quaker family on the beach with bathing machines in the distance

The Seaton Hotel was a popular place to stay, providing accommodation for upper class visitors both in the hotel and in six lodging-houses adjacent to the main building. Parties from Hartlepool, Redcar and Coatham regularly took dinner and/or tea there, and balls were held in its assembly room, which had a gallery and two large chandeliers.

This all sounds very gentle and traditional, but the country was in the latter stages of the Industrial Revolution (1750 – 1850) and there were plenty of developments in engineering and industry in the wider area.

In 1831 when Holy Trinity Church was established at Seaton Carew, William IV was crowned, having taken the throne the previous summer after the death of his elder brother George IV. Earl Grey was Prime Minister. A new London Bridge was opened – the same one that was sold in 1967 and rebuilt in Arizona, with the buyer denying that he thought it was Tower Bridge.

Closer to home, a proposal was being developed for a new railway to make Hartlepool a coal port, taking advantage of the nearby Durham coalfields to ship out minerals. The transformation of Hartlepool from a fishing community into one of Britain's busiest ports was about to take place.

The famous engineer Isambard Kingdom Brunel visited Hartlepool in December 1831 when he came to the north east to bid for work building Monkwearmouth Docks, and took the opportunity to visit several towns examining bridges and other engineering works. He observed it was "*a curiously isolated old fishing town – a remarkably fine race of men. Went to the top of the church tower for a view*". We are not sure which church tower this was.

The establishment of the railway and a station at Seaton had a notable impact on the village. Instead of the well-off gentry being the only ones able to visit Seaton, this pleasure was available to the masses, and they visited in droves. The railway also provided a means of transporting goods, and the timber companies located in Coronation Drive near the sea front did especially well, selling and transporting pit-props for use in the coal mines.

Around the area, iron works and blast furnaces started to be built during the 1840s. These dramatic changes in the landscape do not seem to have encroached on village life in Seaton Carew until later.

In terms of religious buildings, it is known that there once was a chapel in Seaton Carew, dedicated to Thomas à Becket, established some time in the 12th century and lasting until the end of the 16th century. It was certainly in ruins by 1622, but no-one knows exactly where this was. There is speculation that the 13th hole of the golf course that is named Chapel Open might possibly be on this site, and that the greenkeeper's hut may have been erected using the chapel's foundations.

A Methodist Chapel was opened on The Front in 1830 (long since demolished). In those days there was no real barrier between the village and the sands; it is said that on occasions, the waves could be heard splashing against the windows during services.

Prior to 1831, the church at Stranton, near Hartlepool town centre, was the nearest place of worship for Church of England residents of Seaton village. Stranton's burial registers show many interments of people from Seaton, until Holy Trinity had its own churchyard consecrated. The journey to one's final resting place could only be made via a rough track between the two settlements.

At the time of Holy Trinity being built, the population of the village was only around 300, although it would have seemed much busier when the visitors were out and about.

The 19th century nationally was a time of great change, and the established church was trying to keep pace with rapid population growth and significant social and economic changes. The clergy were being placed in a new role, as community leaders, with more social responsibility. The ancient system of parishes, which catered more for the landed gentry and men of influence, had changed very slowly, and needed updating to be able to react more quickly to people's needs. This was a time of rapid growth in both the number of new churches and restoration work on existing churches. There were new church schools, parish halls, and a wide range of clubs for various sections of society.

Holy Trinity was one of 514 new churches built in England between 1831 and 1840, with a further 86 being restored. The government had supported the Church of England with a massive grant of £1m in 1818, badged as a thank offering for the Battle of Waterloo, when Wellington returned having defeated Napoleon. However, none of this fund can have been earmarked for Seaton Carew, because private money was the means by which this little seaside village obtained its own church. The creation of Holy Trinity Church can be considered as the most significant event in the modern history of Seaton Carew.

CHAPTER 2: THE WILKINSON/LAWSON FAMILY

Without the generosity of Barbara Isabella Lawson and George Hutton Wilkinson, it is unlikely that there would be a Church of England church at Seaton Carew. George gave the land and Barbara gave the money to build the church. Barbara (who later became Lady Lawson) also held the patronage. This meant she provided the stipend (salary) for the vicar. As it happened, this was in the family interest: two of her sons held the post of Vicar of Holy Trinity Church.

Barbara Isabella Lawson

George Hutton Wilkinson

George was Recorder (a judge) of Newcastle upon Tyne and Hartlepool during the 1830s. His family seat was at Harperley Park in Durham. Interestingly his daughter Dorothy Wilkinson married Revd. Arthur Duncombe Shafto, the grandson of the famous Bobby Shafto (Robert), who was MP for County Durham between 1760 and 1768. Robert used his nickname "Bonny Bobby Shafto" and the famous song of the same name for electioneering purposes. The lands of Durham and Yorkshire were kept in a closely-spun web of families; the

7

Duncombe name comes from Bobby Shafto's wife Anne, who was the heir to Duncombe Park.

George seems to have owned a fair amount of land and buildings in Seaton, including the farmland all around the church site as well as the Seaton Hotel. It seems that he inherited the hotel through his marriage to Jane Pearson. She was the daughter of George Pearson of Durham, who built it.

George Hutton Wilkinson was also Chairman of the Great North of England Railway (GNER). Members of the Pease and Backhouse families (also active benefactors in Seaton Carew and the area generally), were involved in this company. George was directly responsible for asking George Stephenson to explore the best route for a railway between Newcastle and Edinburgh in 1838.

Barbara Lawson's maiden name was Wilkinson, so there is a strong possibility that she and George Hutton Wilkinson were related. A lengthy search through their respective family trees has not yet unearthed a firm connection. George's diaries have survived and are held in Durham Records Office. Covered in red leather, and with expenses recorded on one side of each page and the week's activities on the other, they reveal that he made visits to Boroughbridge in connection with the elections there and dined with Mr Lawson at Aldborough, so he at least knew Barbara's relatives.

Barbara Isabella was born in 1769, to John Wilkinson (a barrister) and Ellen née Clarke. She married Reverend Marmaduke Lawson, who was 20 years her senior, at Sheffield in 1791. The Lawsons were part of the nobility, able to trace their ancestors back to William the Conqueror.

Barbara's husband Marmaduke was the Rector of Sproatley and Prebendary of Ripon, and the first promoter of schools for religious education in Aldborough parish. He was said to be an able but very reserved man. The tradition of a race meeting held in Boroughbridge every October was stopped largely due to his influence, as he felt that the money was better spent on education. In 1812 the races ceased, and later a school was opened maintained by private subscriptions formerly given for the racing, as well as weekly payments from parents. This influence obviously extended to the two clergymen sons of the family, James and John, as both were avid supporters of education.

The Yorkshire Wilkinsons from whom Barbara was descended also belonged to the nobility and owned Boroughbridge Hall and Aldborough Manor. The Manor included the towns of Aldborough, Boroughbridge and

Minskip. Barbara's uncle, Revd. James Wilkinson, was the vicar of Sheffield for 50 years. As he was the last of the Wilkinson line when he died unmarried in 1805, he left his estates at Boroughbridge to his niece and her family the Lawsons. This included Boroughbridge Hall.

Boroughbridge Hall

We are not sure how Barbara Lawson came to have an interest in Seaton Carew and become the beneficiary of the church, but TS Turner's History of Aldborough & Boroughbridge records that her uncle Revd. James Wilkinson had some sort of pulmonary complaint and used to come to Hartlepool to benefit from the sea air. In the year after his death a mail coach started to run from Boroughbridge to Sunderland, which came through Seaton Carew. This may have been how Barbara and her family got to know the area and later to own land there.

Barbara and Marmaduke had eight children:

1.   Mary Lawson, born c.1791, who married Revd. Alexander Steward.

2.   Marmaduke Lawson, born 1793, who won a fellowship at Cambridge and became MP for Boroughbridge; died unmarried in 1823 aged 30.

3.   Barbara, born 1796, died unmarried in 1859.

4.   Andrew, born 1800, MP for Knaresborough, who married Marianne Gooch and had 10 children; died in 1853.

5.   Dorothy (Dora), born 1802, who married Revd. Edward Bird the curate of Boroughbridge. Dora set up a Sunday school in Boroughbridge. She

died in 1866. Dora and Edward had two daughters, the eldest being Isabella Lucy Bird, who travelled to the East and America, and wrote a series of books about her travel experiences.

6.   Elizabeth b 1805.

7.   James (the first priest-in-charge of Seaton Carew) born 1806, died in 1872.

8.   John (the third priest-in-charge/vicar of Seaton Carew) born 1807, died in 1890.

Barbara lived as a widow for 23 years after her husband's death in 1815, and died at Seaton Carew in 1838. She was well loved and seems to have been quite a strong character. Her husband believed that had she been given the chance, Barbara would have made an even better way in life than her sons. After her death, the patronage of the church passed to other members of her family, thus retaining the Lawson family interest.

When their eldest son Marmaduke was considering giving up his parliamentary seat in 1819 because he felt a failure, Barbara tried to change his mind. She canvassed so effectively for him that he was re-elected, although he was regarded by many as a joker and an eccentric. In 1819 Edward John Littleton recorded in his diary *"Attended the House when Mr Lawson, a mad Member of Parliament made a laughable speech on presenting a petition for leave to bring in a turnpike bill"*. An obituary claims that his "ludicrous oratory will not soon be forgotten".

A document has survived from 1823 which records a guarantee that Marmaduke would repay to Barbara Isabella Lawson *"the sum of twelve thousand pounds of good and lawful money"*, this being the amount she had handed over to ensure he could contest the seat at the parliamentary elections. This was a huge sum of money in those days; only a mother could turn a blind eye to Marmaduke's faults and hand it over. Fortunately Marmaduke's younger brothers James and John had a more earnest and caring attitude.

Isabella Bird, Barbara's granddaughter, was a fascinating character, appearing to inherit some of Barbara's determination. Coincidentally she was born in 1831, the year Holy Trinity was consecrated, but it is safe to say she was certainly ahead of her time and did not conform to the role expected of a lady of her status. She found the lifestyle in her father Revd. Bird's vicarage too stifling, and embarked on travels when a change of air was recommended as a cure during a period of ill health. She had no formal schooling but was educated by her mother Dora.

One of the most celebrated and influential female travel writers of the Victorian era, Isabella was also an explorer, missionary, journalist, and author, who travelled around many countries all over the world, often on horseback. Her choice of companion for her adventures through America was an enigmatic one-eyed outlaw named Jim Nugent, who loved poetry, but who probably provided a challenge for Isabella, as he was an alcoholic and she had a mission to stop people drinking themselves to death. He was shot dead a year after Isabella left the Rockies.

This amazing lady published ten books about her travels, numerous articles, and two books of photographs. She was the first western woman to travel up the Yangtze River or climb Mauna Lao in Hawaii (the largest volcano on earth at the time). Her written accounts of the assassination of the Korean Queen and Japan's invasion of Korea were considered major news stories.

Isabella Bird married late in life in 1881 aged 50, just after her sister's death. Tragically her husband Dr John Bishop died of anaemia only 5 years later, which prompted her to undertake further travelling. Her achievements were not fully recognised until 1892, when she was invited to become the first woman fellow of the prestigious Royal Geographical Society at the age of 61. She was also the first woman Fellow of the Royal Scottish Geographical Society in Edinburgh. She died in 1904 and is commemorated on a blue heritage plaque on the Boroughbridge Hall gatepost.

Isabella Lucy Bird, granddaughter of Barbara Lawson

Seaton was very fortunate in being chosen to benefit from the Lawson family's generosity. They spotted a need in this growing seaside resort and were in a position to use their fortune to help the community develop and thrive.

CHAPTER 3: THE CREATION
OF HOLY TRINITY CHURCH

The ceremony of the laying of a foundation stone for Holy Trinity was reported in the York Herald and General Advertiser on Saturday, March 19, 1831:

"New Church at Seaton Carew, Durham

On Wednesday last, the foundation stone of a new church was laid at this delightfully romantic watering place, amidst the firing of cannon and the rejoicings of the inhabitants. The procession (accompanied by an excellent band from Stockton and Hartlepoole), proceeded from White's Hotel to the site; when after reading the 95th psalm, the stone was laid, in which was deposited a plate containing the following inscription:

This first stone of

Holy Trinity Church,

Was laid this 16th day of March, Anno Domini 1831,

By George Hutton Wilkinson,

Of Harperley Park, in the County of Durham, Esq.

Who gave the Site,

Having been liberally endowed by Barbara Isabella Lawson,

of Boroughbridge Hall, in the County of York, gentlewoman;

the patronage of the living is vested in the said Barbara

Isabella Lawson, and her heirs for ever.

Thos. Pickersgill, Architect.

Mr Wilkinson having addressed the assembled spectators, an appropriate prayer was offered by the Revd. J. Brewster, sen., after which a select party dined together at the Hotel, and in the evening, about 100 children were regaled on tea and cakes, at the expense of Mrs Lawson."

This was obviously a cause for great celebration, although it is notable that there was a social division between the "select party" who went on to a dinner (doubtless at the Seaton Hotel owned by George Hutton Wilkinson), and the rest of the villagers who were left to mark the occasion in their own way. However, we can imagine that Mrs Lawson's kind gesture of tea and cakes for the children would have gone down well.

George Hutton Wilkinson's diaries show that he made several visits to Seaton before the foundation stone ceremony, for the setting out of the site for the chapel, and the laying of the foundations. He dined with Rev Lawson and also with Mr Pickersgill the architect. On another occasion he came to shoot at Seaton, bagging 4 brace of partridge and a hare.

There is no sign of a foundation stone in the current building. As the church was extended in 1842, it is possible that this was on the east wall of the nave and that it was removed when the chancel was built. However, a closer look at the description of the stone in the newspaper report suggests the stone was unmarked; it was the plate hidden inside that was inscribed. It is therefore possible that it is lying concealed somewhere within the current building, as a time capsule. This is the first of several mysteries in the church's history, which may never be solved.

Barbara Isabella Lawson gave the money for the church to be built, and local people helped with the organisation of the building project. In July 1831 John Brewster, who had been vicar at Greatham and was now at Egglescliffe, wrote to the Trustees of Lord Crewe's charity asking for assistance in completing the church. He informed them that the cost of the building was originally estimated at £500, but due to the stone at Seaton not being suitable, they had to obtain it from Hartlepool. This increased the cost to £700, and although subscriptions had been invited, there was still a gap of £100 to find.

John Brewster's letter estimates completion by September. As this was achieved, one assumes that his plea was successful. However, further funds must have been found on top of this, because the final construction cost was £819.19s.5d.

The architect for the church was Thomas Pickersgill (1807-1869), who later became City Architect, Engineer and Surveyor of York. The original building consisted of the western tower and the nave, built from magnesian limestone and honey coloured sandstone. It seated 260 people, in dark pews and benches, with a simple table as an altar, and plain leaded glass in the windows. Mackenzie and Ross's history of Durham County records that the east window of the nave comprised three pointed lights.

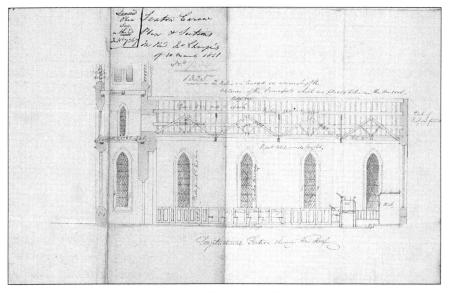

Pickersgill exterior plan

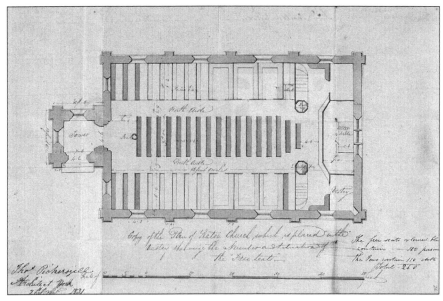

Pickersgill interior floor plan

The copies of the original plans are reproduced with the kind permission of the Trustees of Lambeth Palace Library.

One of the best features of the architectural design of Holy Trinity is its openness; there are no internal pillars, providing good natural light and a clear view of the stained glass windows on the north and south sides.

The consecration of the church took place on the Festival of St Michael and All Angels, 29th September 1831, by Bishop Van Mildert, the last of the Prince Bishops of Durham. On the following Sunday, a sermon was preached at the service of Holy Communion by the Revd. John Brewster, Rector of Egglescliffe, on "The Duty and Advantage of attending the Divine Services of the Church".

One of the perks of being the patron of the living was that Barbara Lawson could install her son James as the first priest-in-charge. This term was used rather than vicar, due to the fact that in its early days, Seaton's church was a chapel within the parish of Stranton.

Revd. James Lawson – Priest in charge 1831 – 1833

James Lawson came to Seaton Carew in 1831 at the age of 25, just after achieving his MA from Oxford. He only stayed for two years, after which he became vicar of Buckminster, Leicestershire. It must have been quite daunting to a newly ordained clergyman to be expected to establish a new church, but one can imagine that his mother would have provided plenty of advice and guidance. Sadly his father Marmaduke had died in 1815.

Among the church's silverware is a chalice inscribed in Latin, revealing that it was given by James Lawson in 1831 for use in the church of Holy Trinity Seaton Carew. It includes the inscription AMDG, which stands for Ad Maiorem Dei Gloriam, "For the greater glory of God". I held this chalice in my hands 181 years later, thinking of the people who have handled it over the years, and feeling a great sense of history.

After he left Holy Trinity, James published a collection of poems in 1842 dedicated to his brother John and their sister Mary, in order to

James Lawson chalice 1831

15

raise money to build a chapel at Buckminster. James and John were close; both were at Oxford University (St Alban Hall) together.

James was the victim of a theft in 1836 at Buckminster, when some lamb's wool stockings of his were stolen from a hedge where they had presumably been left out to dry. The thief was sentenced to two months' imprisonment with hard labour. Sentencing appears to have been rather harsh in those days, but the revelation of what a vicar wore under his cassock gives the story an interesting slant!

Revd. Arthur Guinness – Priest in charge 1833 – 1835

Many people do not realise that the second priest in charge of Holy Trinity (before it became a parish in its own right) was not James' brother John Lawson, but the Reverend Arthur Guinness, who was part of the famous brewing dynasty from Ireland.

Arthur was the grandson of Arthur Guinness, who founded the brewery at St James' Gate in Dublin. Arthur senior was a man of faith, influenced by John Wesley (whom he saw preach at St Patrick's Cathedral in Dublin) into using his wealth to help people. He showed great care and concern for his employees at the Guinness brewery, founded the first Sunday schools in Ireland and gave vast sums of money to the poor.

Arthur senior had 10 children, the second eldest being Hosea Guinness, who became an ordained minister and was Rector of St Werburgh's in Dublin for 30 years. Hosea married Jane Hart and had 12 children. Holy Trinity's Arthur was their second child (and their first son), born in 1796 in Dublin, and destined to become one of a large number of clergy in the Guinness family.

Revd. Guinness' first post was as Curate at Loughall, County Antrim in Ireland. He is named in the Report of the Society for Promoting the Education of the Poor in 1824, as being an applicant for Chapelizod Parochial School in Dublin. Seaton Carew seems to have attracted clergy with a strong interest in education. In 1831 he married Catherine Laughton Paul, who was herself the daughter of a clergyman. This history is littered with many examples of marriages between vicars and daughters of clergymen, possibly because anyone committing themselves to the position of a vicar's wife in those days really needed to know what they were letting themselves in for. They were expected to play a substantial unpaid role in the church in all sorts of ways, particularly in supporting the ladies of the parish in various societies and doing good works. By 1832 Arthur was vicar of St Thomas' Church Dublin.

In 1833 Revd. Guinness became priest in charge of Holy Trinity. It has not been possible to find any explanation as to why he came to England, much less how he ended up at Seaton Carew. Arthur and Catherine had 6 children: Jane, Mary, Margaret, Anne Elizabeth, Arthur Hart, and Thomas Hosea Guinness.

There are many versions of the Guinness family history, but little mention of Seaton Carew's Revd. Arthur Guinness. The focus tends to be on his more famous brewer, banker and missionary relatives, including Henry Grattan Guinness, a famous preacher. I contacted Michelle Guinness, who wrote an excellent history of the family, "The Guinness Spirit: Brewers, Bankers, Ministers and Missionaries", to see if she had any further information about Arthur. She was kind enough to search through her extensive collection of books on the Guinness family, but could not find any further information about Revd. Arthur Guinness.

In 1834 Pigot's Directory was published, one of the trade directories which were published periodically with information at a parish level. Seaton Carew was described as "*a pleasant bathing village, situated upon the borders of the sea, and chiefly consisting of neat cottages, forming three sides of a quadrangle; it contains a good inn (the 'Seaton Carew Hotel'), and a row of convenient lodging-houses. The prospects around here are beautiful and extensive. The township contained, by the last returns, 333 inhabitants.*"

Occupations at this time included a baker (John Corner), bathkeeper (James Lithgo), blacksmith (Christopher Bell), boot and shoe makers (Shutt and Weastell), Milliner/dressmakers (Elizabeth Appleton and Ann Lithgo), a librarian (of a circulating library – Jane Ellenor, who also ran a shop), and a grocer (John Pattison).

Like his predecessor, Arthur Guinness only served at Holy Trinity for 2 years, which perhaps explains why there is little record of his time here. He died in 1835 at the age of 39 and is buried in a stone tomb in the crypt at Christ Church on the Stray at Harrogate. The only evidence of him being connected with this part of Yorkshire is information from a member of Christ Church that he used to preach at Knaresborough. There is a tablet on the wall of Christ Church containing a memorial inscription.

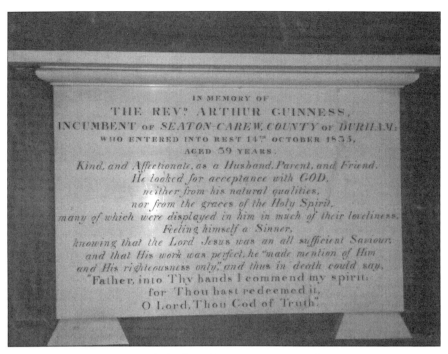

Revd. Arthur Guinness memorial

Research has established that this tablet was created by one of the Fisher family who were well known sculptors of the early 19th century.

Revd. Guinness' death led to the installation of the second Lawson brother to serve as vicar at Holy Trinity, John Lawson.

CHAPTER 4 – REVEREND JOHN LAWSON: DEVOTED SERVANT 1835 – 1890

John Lawson's ministry lasted for a remarkable 55 years. He had a huge influence, not only on the church at Seaton, but also on the education of local children, playing a key role in creating the school and later enlarging it.

Coming from a family of landed gentry, he was in the fortunate position of not having to rely on the stipend of £60 per annum for his living. Moreover, he used his wealth to positively benefit Holy Trinity.

Whenever funds were being raised for any development, Revd. Lawson contributed at least £50, and subscription lists that have survived

Sketch of a young
John Lawson

show he usually made up any shortfall personally. He put his heart and soul into this place, and we and generations of Seatonians have cause to be very grateful for his generosity.

As a child, John Lawson attended Shrewsbury School, was a friend of Charles Darwin and knew Cardinal Newman. After studying Classics at Oxford, he was ordained in 1831 by Bishop Van Mildert, Bishop of Durham. He married Mary Crowe from Stockton in around 1835, and was appointed to Holy Trinity Seaton Carew in December of the same year, after Revd. Arthur Guinness

Revd. John Lawson
in later years

died. He had been in Seaton Carew for two years when Queen Victoria ascended to the throne.

John and Mary had six children born in quick succession: John (1836), Mary (1837), Barbara Isabella (1838), Marmaduke Alexander (1840), Margaret (1841) and Frances Jane (1844). Marmaduke became a famous botanist and died in India. Margaret and Mary did not marry and lived together at Knaresborough. Both Barbara and Frances married clergymen: Barbara's husband was Revd. James Scarlett, and Frances' was Revd. Henry Gott Kinnear. There were a lot of clergy in the Lawson family! Both marriages took place at Seaton Carew, and were presided over by different vicars so that Revd. Lawson could enjoy each ceremony as the father of the bride.

John Lawson came to Seaton at a time when the villagers were keen to keep the local area well serviced. In 1838 they arranged for a summons to be served against the surveyors of the highways for Seaton Carew, for neglect of duty in not keeping them in repair; the penalty for this was £5. The roads were only basic tracks to start off with, so any maintenance problems would be quite an issue. As we will see later, this was an early example of Seatonians expecting things to be done properly.

On 21st October 1841 the Chapelry of Seaton Carew was created and licensed under the Bishop of Durham. This meant that baptisms, weddings, burials and churchings (blessings of women after childbirth) could be carried out there, and the fees from these services were paid to the Minister.

A vicarage was built in 1837 in the north-west corner of the church grounds, designed by the famous architect Anthony Salvin. This replaced the original parsonage in Church Street. The entrance bore an inscription "Non Nobis Domine", a reference to a short hymn:

"Non nobis, non nobis domine, Sed nomini tuo da Gloriam"
"Not to us, not to us, O Lord, but to your name give glory".

Salvin (1799-1881) was born in Sunderland and specialised in church architecture, both new buildings and restoration, but also designed manors, country houses and castles. He designed Moreby Hall in Yorkshire, Thoresby Hall in Nottingham (now a Warner's holiday resort), and the monument to Grace Darling in Bamburgh. It is a great pity that the Seaton vicarage was left to deteriorate in the 20th century and was demolished in 1977, but it would have been a huge drain on the church's resources. Considerable time was spent at PCC meetings debating its future, until the Bishop insisted something had to be done. Its disappearance was lamented by experts in architecture and fans of Salvin.

The following photograph of an early drawing includes the vicarage. This is the first of several photographs included which were taken by Revd. Pattison, a curate at Holy Trinity from 1885 – 1890; permission to reproduce them here has kindly been granted by Bowes Museum. The Pattison collection of photographs can be viewed on their website, www.bowesmuseum.org.uk. The collection represents a fascinating record of social history from the late 19th century.

Church before extension – drawing photographed by Revd. Pattison

Revd. Lawson was very active in the early years of his ministry, and had a clear vision. He developed the church and introduced activities that would serve the villagers well for succeeding generations. It did not take long before he felt it necessary to make plans to extend the church, starting up a subscription list to invite donations for this purpose.

The initial circular issued in 1841 showed that the vicar had thought about giving the maximum publicity to his plans, using contacts outside the local area to help him seek the necessary funding:

CHURCH EXTENSION
SEATON-CAREW

"The Church at Seaton Carew, which was built AD 1831, and contains 260 sittings, though still sufficiently large for the resident population, has for some time past been inadequate, during the Bathing Season, for the joint accommodation of the Visitors and Inhabitants.

Since the period of its erection Seaton has greatly increased in size (an addition having been every year made to the number of Lodging Houses) and in consequence of the recent opening of the Stockton and Hartlepool Railway, which affords a ready access from the interior of the country to the Sea coast, there is every prospect that it will in future increase yet more rapidly. Under these circumstances it becomes evidently necessary to provide increased Church Accommodation, and with a view to effect this object a Plan has been drawn, which has received the sanction of the Bishop of the Diocese and the Archdeacon of Durham. By this plan it is proposed to enlarge the Church by erecting a Chancel and Gallery, and thus to secure 246 new sittings, of which number 140 are intended to be free and unappropriated. With this addition the Church will hold upwards of 500 persons, and the total number of free sittings in it will be 290.

It is proposed, at the same time, to enlarge the Church Yard (which is at present so contracted as scarcely to be available for Burials) and also to purchase a Clock for the Church Tower, the want of a public Time-piece in the place being felt to be a great inconvenience.

The total cost of these several Improvements is estimated at £550, and to raise this sum an appeal is now made to the friends of Church Extension in general, and more especially to those Families who are in the habit of visiting Seaton during the Bathing Season.

Subscriptions in aid of the above objects will be thankfully received by the Rev I D EADE, Aycliffe Vicarage, Darlington; CAPTAIN DALTON, The Grange, near Ripon; and the Rev J LAWSON, Seaton Carew, or they may be paid into Messrs Backhouse & Co's bank, Durham, Darlington and Stockton. Subscriptions, if desired, may be given specially for the Clock."

It appears that inflation and changes to builders' estimates are not just a modern phenomenon; in 1842 a second circular was published, stating that the costs had increased. While the original estimate of £550 had been raised, the amount now required was no less than £800. The list of subscriptions achieved included £50 each from the Church Building Society and the Diocesan Church Building Society, £25 from the Earl of Eldon and £21 from the Lord Bishop of Durham.

Revd. Lawson not only donated £50 (out-doing his Lord Bishop), but also transferred some of his own land to enable the church yard to be enlarged, and gave £130 for an organ and stained glass windows. He encouraged a good many fellow clergymen to give donations as well as members of his own family (Lawsons and Wilkinsons alike), to minimise the amount required from parishioners. Being from a reputable and affluent family brought great benefits on such occasions.

Other avenues were also explored to raise funds; the York Herald of 9th July 1842 reported that:

"On Sunday last, two sermons were preached in the church at Seaton Carew; in the morning by the Rev H Jenkyns, DD., canon of Durham, and in the afternoon by the Rev J Lawson, incumbent. After each sermon, a collection was made towards defraying the expenses caused by the erection of a gallery and chancel, amounting to £17 18s."

The effect of the extension can be seen in the following etching by the architect, showing the familiar shape of the church we know and love today. It is noticeable that the East window is deeper than the current window, and that there were no adjoining buildings at that time. The church was still surrounded by farmland.

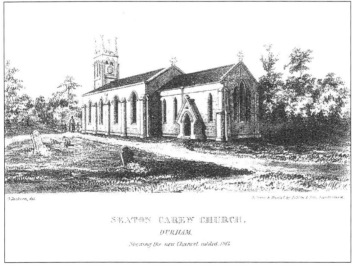

Jackson etching 1842

The final accounts held in Durham Records Office show the final cost of the extension as £806 15s 2d, almost as much as the original building cost. The subscriptions raised did not fully cover this, leaving a shortfall of £35 8s 5d. Revd. Lawson paid the remaining sum out of his own means, which often happened, according to later records. The architect was George Jackson, a local man William Walker was the joiner, and the clock was made by Samuel Thompson of Darlington.

The account for the organ, which was installed in the new gallery, describes it as follows:

"Joseph Walker organ builder of Francis Street Tottenham Court Road £63 1s for a Barrel Organ with 3 barrels playing 10 tunes each in one frame, in neat painted Gothic Case, 9 feet high, 5 feet wide and 3 feet deep.

With Gill Pipes in the front, containing the following stops:

Double Diapason Bass

Open Diapason

Principal

Fifteenth"

This description suggests that the congregation only had a choice of 30 hymns. Perhaps this limitation explains why the organ only lasted six years before it was enlarged, by James Nicholson of Newcastle, at a much higher cost: £78 10s.

The east window was designed and produced by William Wailes from Newcastle. Born in 1808, he initially set up in business as a high-class grocer. Having built up enough capital, in 1836 he opened a showroom and stained glass factory in the Central Exchange Building in Newcastle, advertising stained glass at a readily affordable price. It had previously been viewed as a luxury, but the Gothic Revival had reintroduced mosaic style glazing and the medieval style of painting, which provided an opportunity for cost-competitive manufacture on a large scale. Despite this, many of the windows produced by Wailes are considered as art, such as those at St Mary's RC Cathedral in Newcastle and Ely Cathedral.

By 1851 the business had become one of the largest stained glass studios outside of London, producing windows for churches and houses throughout the British Empire and North America.

The agreement with William Wailes, dated 9th April 1842, to execute the stained glass altar window can be seen as a very clear instruction to secure good value for money and a timely installation:

"I William Waile of Newcastle upon Tyne do hereby undertake to execute in stained glass the altar window of Seaton Carew Church of the present size in the manner of the five sisters at York – of the best possible workmanship on double thick glass for the sum of sixty pounds – also the 3 south windows in the chancel with an Early English pattern on each quarry and ornamental border. And to curtain one of these ornaments as required for the sum of ten pounds additional, the whole to be fixed in their proper situations for the above sum and the whole to be fixed by the 1st day of June next."

The "five sisters at York" refers to the oldest complete window in York Minster, which dates from 1260. This was in the "grisaille" style, which involved painting foliage patterns on to white or silvery grey glass. The pieces were then formed into strong geometric patterns using lead "cames" to hold the pieces together.

There are several theories about why the York Minster window bears the Five Sisters name, including a story in Dickens' Nicholas Nickleby about five sisters who, on the death of one sister, commissioned the window in the Minster as a memorial. Alternatively it may be a corruption of Five Cistercians, because the characteristic grisaille glass was popular with the Cistercian Order. Some of this style of glass can be seen today in part of the window on the north wall of the nave of Holy Trinity, which is dedicated to Anna and Jane Wray, the earliest of the memorial windows we see today.

Reconstructions of the heavily corroded Five Sisters window at York were only published in 1847, so Wailes must have relied on his own templates. He may have made some during his restoration work at the Minster following the fire of 1840.

The three windows in the south wall of the chancel also referred to in the commissioning agreement with William Wailes are interesting. The description in the order to Wailes tells us these windows originally had an ornamental border, but this is not present in today's windows. Two of them were damaged by shrapnel during the Second World War, and by the 1980s, they were in a very poor condition. Revd. Worley engaged Leonard Evetts in 1983 to design new windows, re-using the central medallions. Elders Walker and Millican Ltd installed the windows. This was funded by a legacy from the mother-in-law of Nat Abrams the Town Clerk of Hartlepool.

Leonard Evetts also designed the Stella Maris window in Durham Cathedral's Galilee Chapel, which contains Bede's tomb. This was installed in 1993, funded by a donation by the American Friends of Durham Cathedral.

The church has a photographic record of the original chancel windows, shown on page 85.

These windows contain depictions of Jesus as Salvator Mundi (Saviour of the World), St Peter, and St Paul. The photographs on page 86 show close up views of the three medallions set in Leonard Evetts' windows.

The Salvator Mundi pose is identical to that in a Leonardo Da Vinci painting of the same name, which was believed to be lost but was newly discovered in 2011 and verified as a genuine Da Vinci. Jesus has his hand raised in a benediction pose and in his left hand he holds an orb, representing the world.

St Peter holds two keys, symbols derived from St Matthew's Gospel Chapter 16, verses 18-20: *"And I tell you, you are Peter, and on this rock I will build my church, and the gates of Hades will not prevail against it. I will give you the keys of the kingdom of heaven, and whatever you bind on earth will be bound in heaven, and whatever you loose on earth will be loosed in heaven."*

St Paul holds a sword; there are two theories about this. One is derived from the letter of Paul to the Ephesians, Chapter 6 verse 17: *"Take the helmet of salvation, and the sword of the Spirit, which is the Word of God."* The second theory is that it represents the sword by which Paul died. As a Roman citizen, he could not be crucified or stoned; he was therefore given the "honour" of being beheaded.

The new burial ground was consecrated by the Bishop of Durham on 26th July 1842. Afterwards the Revd. Dr Hook, vicar of Leeds, preached a sermon.

Between 1840 and 1843, Revd. Lawson must have seized the opportunity to purchase additional land next to the vicarage, because the Church's ownership increased from 16 acres to 38 ½ acres.

Records of the church accounts between 1832 and 1852 give an insight into what the church interior was like and how it was run. Pew rents generated £24 in 1832 and £34 by 1843, but declined after this. In 1844, 5½ gallons of oil were purchased for the chancel walls, presumably to keep the original wooden panelling nourished. The unpanelled walls were whitewashed. Fred Robinson the bellows blower was paid 5s, to keep the organ going, and candles were purchased for the organ so the organist could see the music. Other people were paid for various tasks such as winding up the clock, acting as clerk, and washing surplices. The vicar's wife was paid as sextoness, a post responsible for looking after the graveyard and church maintenance.

In 1844, Revd. Lawson turned his attention to the children of the village and in particular their education, laying the foundations for many future generations to realise their potential.

CHAPTER 5 - THE NATIONAL SCHOOL, 1844

L ong before the introduction of compulsory education in 1870, Revd. Lawson had recognised the need for a school in the village, and in 1843 he started to make plans to build one. Generations of Seaton children have benefited from this single decision by a man who had the interests of all young people at heart, whatever background they came from.

The first day school in Seaton Carew had been created in the 1700s by Lord Nathaniel Crewe, former Bishop of Durham (1674-1721), who gave a grant of £5 per year for the setting up and maintaining of a grammar school in the village. This was at 20 The Cliffe in the low single storey house (now whitewashed) just north of The Green. The Lord Crewe charity still exists.

Early histories mention that the day school was not particularly well attended, because the poor were reliant upon the free instruction received at the Sunday School held in the vicarage for 27 boys and 30 girls. A daily school was also held in a parish school room. It is not clear where this was, but as we will see later, it was not fit for purpose.

There were other schools on The Green, especially during the latter part of the 19th century, but as boarding schools they would not have catered

Single storey original school building on The Cliff, north of The Green

for the poor of Seaton. They included St Joseph's Academy (a catholic school for boys) in the 1870s, Mrs Maria and Miss Mary Cowper's seminary for young ladies at numbers 3 and 3A The Green (1873 to 1887), Mr & Mrs Ramsey's girls school (1884-6), and Misses Haraap and Sterndale girls' school (1900 onwards) which was created by combining the two large houses on the west corner of North Road. There is a Sterndale Trust which has lasted for many years and still provides scholarships for young musicians, with award winners performing at an annual concert, which is organised by Holy Trinity's current organist Derryck Pinfield.

In November 1843 Revd. Lawson gathered together the principal inhabitants of Seaton Carew to discuss a proposal "*to build a large and commodious school with a House for a Master attached, to be legally secured in perpetuity for the Education of Children residing in the Chapelry of Seaton Carew, and having given a site in a very eligible situation for this purpose, on condition that the present school room and house are disposed of, and the proceeds applied towards the cost of erecting the new buildings*".

The group of people, who appear to have been mainly local landowners, evidently with self-imposed status and authority, gave their consent.

By the following January, the plans took a step further with the completion of a questionnaire outlining the proposals more fully. This document, written in John Lawson's own hand, provides a well thought-out description of the project. The plot of land was glebe land (belonging to the Living of Seaton Carew, i.e. the vicar), on Ashburn Street, bounded by the parsonage gardens to the north and west, and Church Street to the south. The building was to be of brick, with six windows of zinc casements, and a slate roof. Boys and girls had separate yards.

The trustees were to be the Minister, Chapelwardens and Overseers of the Poor of the Chapelry of Seaton Carew. The Poor Laws made the care and supervision of the poor a responsibility of each town or village. Each Easter a parish was required to appoint two Overseers, who were responsible for setting the poor rate, its collection and the relief of those in need.

John Lawson secured a grant of £5 per annum for the new school from Lord Crewe's Trustees and the Bishop of Durham was reported in the press as giving a "*liberal donation of twenty guineas to a fund for building a national school at Seaton Carew*". The National School Society gave £120, a substantial amount in those days. Revd. Lawson also pledged a personal donation of £15 per year and £10 annually from church collections. The new school was intended to educate up to 84 girls and 84 boys, charging fees to those families who could afford them, at least when they remembered to pay – there does not seem to have been much debt collecting undertaken.

Revd. Lawson pulled no punches in setting out the rationale as to why a new school was needed:

"Schools existing:

Sunday school taught in the Parsonage – attendance boys 27, girls 30. Many more children would attend this school, if there were accommodation for them.

Daily School, taught in the Parish School Room, a very mean & miserable building, inconveniently situated, and utterly incapable of improvement. Attendance boys 16, girls 10 – accommodation for 36 children at the utmost. It is intended to sell this building, and apply the proceeds (estimated at £100) to the erection of the new school.

Daily School, taught in a private house, attendance boys 20, girls 10.

Grounds for representing this case as deserving of assistance – the rapid increase of the population. The great want of a good school at Seaton Carew. The anxious desire of the inhabitants to possess one. The liberal manner in which contributions have been given for this purpose. The certainty that the school, when established, will be efficiently and permanently supported, because the incumbent and his friends & parishioners generally take a great interest in their success, and are determined to maintain them in an efficient manner."

Source: Durham Record Office EP/SC11/5

Considering the old school was described so disparagingly, they did well to raise over £111 from its sale, although there is no record of who was brave enough to purchase it.

The school was completed at a total cost of £656 9s 4d, and there was a shortfall of just over £41, so additional subscriptions had to be raised. Even after this, there was still a deficiency of £9 16s 3d. As the builder Mr Walker, who happened to be a church warden, died before the school opened, it is not certain whether the executors of his estate simply had to accept the lower sum, or whether they achieved a full settlement of the bill.

Having invested a lot of time and money, Revd. Lawson understandably wanted to take more than a passing interest in the new school. He stipulated that the school should be under the management and control of the vicar in perpetuity, giving him the ability to hire and fire the Schoolmaster and Schoolmistress. However, this was for the best of reasons: he intended to ensure that the school was always in line with the principles of the National Society for promoting the education of the poor in the principles of the Established Church. The National Society today guides around 4,700 Church of England schools.

The subjects to be taught as a minimum at the National School were reading, writing, arithmetic, geography, scripture, history, and for girls, needlework. It was a fundamental regulation and practice that the children should read the Bible daily, so that all were educated in the principles of the Christian Religion. The first roll comprised 16 boys and 10 girls, taught by Mr Durban and Miss Whitehead. Revd. Lawson must have been quite demanding of the headmasters, as there were 14 of them in the first 46 years of the school, and only two managed to survive for more than two or three years.

The National school was inspected in 1853, by Revd. D J Stewart, a government inspector, a reminder that external assessment of schools is nothing new. His report shows that there were 45 boys and 45 girls present at examination, with average attendance of 36 and 33 respectively. A description of the school is included, recording that it consisted of one fair-sized room with a curtain to separate the boys from the girls, and a stone floor. Desks were grouped in threes, with a stove, clock and book closet as the only other furniture, apart from three blackboards with easels. The playground was a small yard.

The sense of Revd. Lawson's control over the school is reinforced by a letter sent to the trustees of Lord Crewe's charity in 1856, relating to the annual grant of £5 per year for the school. Revd. Lawson reported that the previous school master, William Burrill, had died and he wanted the charity to confirm that they would continue to pay the grant *"to a successor of my own appointing. I am anxious that this limitation should be made in the appropriation of the grant, because it will prevent the intrusion of persons whom I do not think fit for the situation, until I meet with someone who will fill it with credit and advantage to the place."*

Revd. Lawson pledged that if the grant were continued under these conditions, he would give £5 per year himself, and raise another £5 in subscriptions from others, so that with the payments from scholars, a good master would have an income of £30 to £40 per year. He anticipated that the parish would be willing to give the house and schoolroom, which belonged to the township of Seaton, to a schoolmaster appointed by himself, but felt that he would have more influence in the matter if he was able to state that the annual grant would only be paid to someone of his choice. He did, however, ask the trustees if they knew of anyone *"of good capacity for teaching, zeal, piety and attachment to the Church"* who might undertake the role.

However, the children and their parents did not have a particularly respectful appreciation of the school. Lateness and absenteeism were frequent, as there often seemed to be more important things to be done such as fishing, helping out on their relatives' farms with potato picking and haymaking, looking after the cows, clearing up shipwrecks, shrimping, gathering sea coal, and other errands. Some boys worked, notably caddying for golfers at the local golf club when matches took place. On one occasion a parent sent a message to say that a pupil would be absent because the lessons were too hard!

The children who lived at the cottages near the Zinc Works south of Seaton had a perfect excuse to finish the school day early at a particular time of year: they had to get across the land (called Wideopen) before the spring tides cut them off. Other children met with trouble; the village policeman came for two boys who had been stealing apples from someone's garden, and the school master had to punish some boys for putting gunpowder in the fire.

Absences got so bad that in 1878 a school attendance officer was appointed, but apparently this had little effect. By 1921 the school started to admit scholars from the newly built village of Graythorp, but their attendance was no better. The school log book records *"Graythorp children come when they please, Seaton children do not require much bad weather to frighten them."* There was also a complaint that the infants' standards were poor due to the Graythorp children's academic performance. However, by 1926 Graythorp had its own school, causing numbers to decline at Seaton School.

Illnesses were also frequent: diphtheria, glandular fever, measles, chickenpox, ringworm, typhoid and scarlet fever. On more than one occasion the school had to be closed and disinfected to remove all traces of infection, otherwise the parents would have refused to send their children.

The 1876 accounts for the National School have survived, and show how funding was secured for the running costs. Fees were paid by the children, referred to as "School Pence", which generated around £60 per year. There were collections after sermons, grants from The Committee of Council, Betton's Charity and Lord Crewe's Trustees, and annual subscriptions from individuals, again demonstrating John Lawson's talent for persuasion. The vicar not only gave £15 per year, but also made up the overall shortfall in income of £18 from his own pocket. The expenditure records show that equal pay had not been invented – the school master was paid £103 2s 9d but the school mistress only received £62 18s 8d. As with many schools today, the next highest item was the running costs of the building: coal and gas, repairs and cleaning.

Revd. Lawson was treasurer of the school, and he and his mother paid subscriptions every year. Revd. Lawson's determination to provide the children of Seaton Carew with a good education did not wane even in his later years. In 1883 he set up another appeal to fund additional classrooms at the school. The enlargement to create a new school room in 1884, built by William Cockburn of West Hartlepool, provided sufficient space to take 70 infants and 70 juniors.

The extended National School, 1888 (now the parish centre);
the original building on Ashburn Street is just visible on the right.
By Revd. Pattison

In 1897 the vicar informed the pupils of the school that they would not be required to pay fees any longer. However, this did not seem to have much impact on attendance – one log book entry in 1917 records that eight children were off to attend a party with Horace Burton's grandmother, eliciting the despairing comment from the school master *"typical attitude of village people"*.

It seems that there was little heating in the school, as one January the master reported that the ink had frozen in the inkwells. Occasionally there were some lighter moments, such as the day that Norman Lithgo brought his goat to school.

It was not just the village school that Rev Lawson was concerned with. In 1874 the local iron industry was started up by J Richardson MP and houses were being built at Long Hill (near St Aidan's), which was part of Seaton Carew parish. The church therefore had a responsibility for this area, and Revd. Lawson decided to build a Mission School in 1874 at a cost of £1000. In 1891 housing growth caused Seaton parish to be split, as it was becoming too large. At this point, the Mission School and the district of Long Hill were transferred to the new parish of St Aidan's.

CHAPTER 6 – DEVELOPMENT OF
SEATON CAREW AS A PARISH

Just after the National School was established, Revd. Lawson was given a golden opportunity to develop Holy Trinity, with a significant improvement in its status. In August 1845 the Church Commissioners wrote to the vicar giving notice of an Act of Parliament which allowed Seaton Carew to become a parish in its own right. He was instructed to appoint the first Churchwardens within two calendar months. Ever one to do things properly, Revd. Lawson made handwritten notes on the reverse of this letter, recording the names of the churchwardens appointed for each of the years between 1845 and 1851.

The first churchwardens were Christopher Harbron and William Robinson – the first being the people's warden and the second the vicar's warden. In 1848 Mr Harbron was replaced by Daniel Taylerson, who was in turn succeeded by John Watt in 1850.

The parishioners did not just think of their own church, but were involved in charitable activities. To raise funds for the Church Missionary Society (CMS) in 1847, sermons were preached at Holy Trinity by the Bishop of Ripon in the morning and by the Revd. G Hodgson of the society in the afternoon. The following evening an annual meeting was held in the National School Room, chaired by Revd. Lawson. These activities raised £27 2s 8d for the CMS charity. Clergy today would probably be flattered to think congregations might pay to hear them preach! By the time of Revd. Lawson's 25th anniversary in 1860, he had helped to raise £2,000 for the CMS.

The School Room was used for a Parish Library, offering a key service to the community. A printer's amended proof from 1847 of the catalogue of 325 books has survived and is held by the Museum of Hartlepool. This shows a fascinating record of reading material that was offered to parishioners. Subscriptions were 1 shilling per year, paid in advance on November 1st. The money received in subscriptions was to be employed in repairs and in the purchase of additional books. A book could be borrowed for a month and the fine was one penny per week for overdue books. The opening hours were limited to 9-10 am on a Monday and 8-9 pm on a Thursday.

As might be expected, the contents of the library were mainly religious books, but there were other subjects – The Solar System, Cowper's Poems, History of the Great Plague, First Book of Geometry, Zoological Sketches, Seaman's Manual, Farmer's Guide to Happiness and Manual for the Aged.

An example of the social activities of the parish arranged to help parishioners while away the cold and dark winter evenings is to be found in the Museum of Hartlepool's collection of documents from Wm Proctor's printing shop: a tea party in 1848.

Tea party poster
by permission of Hartlepool Council's Museum Service

The inhabitants and land owners in Seaton Carew were keen to improve their local area. In September 1848 a public meeting was held in the School Room to discuss how the village could be improved as a "watering place", the quaint Victorian phrase for a seaside resort. It was not just the local residents who attended the meeting, but a large number of people from outside the area, who may have had business interests in Seaton.

A proposal was made to create a sea wall and promenade walk from the north end of the village along the front to the Snook walk or Buoy house at the south end. This would provide a barrier between the houses and the beach, and help to prevent the sands from drifting across. There was no expectation that any public body would provide funding for the new promenade; money was raised by the villagers through subscriptions. They recognised it was in the interests of property owners to fund the improvements, especially those who made a living from providing lodgings for the visitors to Seaton.

The year 1849 saw an outbreak of cholera in Hartlepool, a killer disease which was a common occurrence during the 19th century, particularly in ports. This one was particularly virulent and there seems to have been an attempt at invoking the Lord's assistance through collective prayer, judging by a poster of the time which advertised the following event:

Day of humiliation and prayer

Friday 19th October 1849

To be observed as

A SOLEMN DAY of HUMILIATION AND SPECIAL INTERCESSION

Before ALMIGHTY GOD

In the

PARISHES OF GREATHAM & STRANTON

Including SEATON CAREW

JOHN BREWSTER M.A. VICAR of GREATHAM

ROWLAND WEBSTER M.A. VICAR of STRANTON

JOHN LAWSON M.A. INCUMBENT of SEATON CAREW

By 1851 the population of Seaton was 728, meaning it had more than doubled in just under 20 years. The creation of the Stockton and Hartlepool Railway increased the ability of visitors to make the journey to this seaside resort, with a station just under a mile from the sea front. The newspapers of the time printed reports listing the names of the families who visited Seaton, presumably informed by the lodging-house and hotel owners. The public's interest in the comings and goings of "celebrities" has evidently been going on for longer than we might think.

Whellan's Directory of Durham from 1856 mentions lodging houses, bath houses, bathing machines, and a salmon hatchery as businesses operating at Seaton Carew. The National School was recorded as having 90 children in attendance, taught by Lancelot Reed and Dorothy Glendinning. Lazarus Bowser served as postmaster. There were 13 farmers, occupying farms such as Seaton Grange, Long Hill, Golden Flatts, Tofts, Carr House, Red Barnes, Fence House and Hunter House Farm. Other occupations included lodging house keepers, butcher, iron founder, railway director, blacksmith, joiner, shoemakers, bathkeepers, tailor, magistrate, timber merchant, master mariner, artist, and builder.

In the same year, newspapers carried reports of three young apprentices having drowned while bathing at Seaton. Although the water was shallow, they had been caught in a pool about 10 feet deep, caused by a hole in the sands created from a shipwreck. They had left their clothes in a boat on the shore, because bathing machines were not permitted to operate on a Sunday, which was the only time off the apprentices had. The Coroner recommended that Mr Crawford's bathing machines should be employed on Sundays from 7.00 to 9.00 in the morning and from 1.00 to 3.00 in the afternoon, as this would not interfere with divine service. This indicates the importance of the church in the community, at a time of strict observance of Sunday as a holy day on which businesses should not be open. How times have changed – one wonders what the Victorians would have thought of 24-hour opening.

In March 1860, the parishioners commemorated the 25th year of John Lawson's service. Wishing to recognise *"his sterling character, deep piety and faithful labours as a minister of Christ"*, they set a target to raise £500, with the aim of completing the vicarage by adding a wing. This had been considered when the house was built, but had never been made a reality. The church community felt the vicarage was not spacious enough for his family, and this was probably true given that he had servants, and that the premises were also used for the Sunday School and some church meetings.

The parishioners wanted to organise a real celebration, but recognised that Revd. Lawson did not like ostentatious displays, and therefore settled for a tea party in the National School Room, which was decorated with flags and foliage.

The Stockton & Hartlepool Mercury reported that there was "*an abundant supply of tea and cakes, amongst which latter was a somewhat recherché one imported from Holland, which besides its other merits, was adorned with 25 lighted tapers to commemorate the number of years of the incumbent's residence in Seaton. This was a present from Mrs Fawcus*". This lady, as we will see later, had a husband who often travelled to Europe on business and who must have been given instructions to bring the cake back in time for the celebrations. The guests were entertained with music and several speeches were given. Revd. Lawson was presented with a cheque for the impressive sum of £613 rather than the £500 target.

As a result, an East Wing was added to the vicarage, designed by a local architect Mr W C J West. There must have been a substantial increase in the floor area of the house as a result. An inscription on the East Wall over the study read "This wing was added by the kind munificence of the Friends of the Revd. John Lawson, M.A. to commemorate the 25th year of his Ministry at Seaton Carew, AD 1860. Glory be to Thee O Lord." The plaque can be seen in the following photograph, on the new wing above the first floor window on the right hand side of the building.

Seaton Carew Vicarage

Revd. and Mrs Lawson were also presented with a silver Coffee Pot, Cream Jug and Sugar Basin inscribed as follows:

"*Presented to the Revd John Lawson M.A. and Mrs Lawson as a testimonial of affection from their Parishioners*".

For those in peril on the sea

The lifeboat was another feature of life in Seaton Carew that John Lawson was passionate about, besides the church and the school.

The first lifeboat was given at the beginning of the 19th century by the Backhouse family (who were Quakers) together with a boathouse to keep it in. Although there were many unknown seamen washed up on the beach, there were also many lives saved by the lifeboat and its crew; it is impossible to know how many, but William Hood was awarded the RNLI Silver Medal in 1851 for saving 132 lives in 32 wreck incidents.

A benefactor, William Kerrell of Bath, donated a lifeboat called the Charlotte to Seaton in 1857. He wrote to Revd. Lawson the following year, explaining that:

"My wife, after whom it is named, would like much to know something of the general operation and circumstances of the crew, and if they are mostly married men, what their usual occupations are, but more specifically if they are a sincerely disposed class of men, and if each is supplied with a Bible in good large type. One feels a particular interest in men who may be called at any time to peril their lives for the sake of others, and a desire that they should possess that confidence in God which would give them the highest kind of strength in the face of danger."

Revd. Lawson's reply cannot have given much assurance on the spiritual tendencies of the crew, as the next letter from Mr Kerrell responded that although the account was painful, it did not surprise them, and that they were *"thankful that one out of the sixteen has received the Love of God into his heart"*. This was Robert Hood, who apparently already had a bible.

Not to be discouraged, Mr Kerrell sent 10 bibles and a number of Ryles Tracts and Temperance Tracts. J C Ryle was the first Bishop of Liverpool and wrote evangelical papers. The February edition of the British Workman journal was also sent, Mr Kerrell observing that *"this is a favourite publication among the lower classes, partly on account of the prints, but it is a strong advocate for the Bible as the one book, also for Temperance, and seems to be directed more especially to sailors."* He felt that a weekly Bible class would be beneficial to the men. The next response from Revd. Lawson gave cause for more confidence, indicating the Bibles had been well received. It is a good thing that the crew did not know about Mr Kerrell's disparaging remarks about class, suggesting picture books might be more at their level!

Mr Kerrell also asked for advice from Mrs Lawson to help them get a new cook from the north of England. He ventured the opinion that "*servants are more unsophisticated in the North – in Bath they are sadly injured by the kind of life that is prevalent in a large town – they lead an extremely simple life and there is little cookery required, what we want is a plain cook who can roast and boil well and make plain puddings and who can wash well, although the washings are small – a good tempered, active, obliging person, who can be well recommended from her last place.*" I wonder if he was successful in his search.

Being on the coast with the full blast of winds from the North Sea, there were plenty of occasions when this close-knit community needed to support each other in the face of battles with the elements. In February 1861 a particularly fierce and destructive gale swept the coast, bringing the sea into the streets at quite a depth. Roofs were blown off and windows blown in, with cellars and underground tenements completely flooded. A fleet of ships carrying coal which had just left the port were blown back and 60 vessels were either wrecked or stranded on the beach.

Around fifty people died in the storm; it must have been quite distressing for the villagers to see bodies continuing to be washed up on the beach over the next few days. Sadly shipwrecks were not a rare occurrence. The following photograph shows an example from 1881, the Alphonse Maria.

Wreck of the Alphonse Maria, 1881

To God be the glory

Back on dry land, Revd. Lawson continued to make improvements to the church. In 1864, work was undertaken which included re-pewing, painting, and stoothing, which involved covering a wall in strips of wood and plaster. A total of £245 7s 1d was raised from subscriptions. As usual, Revd. Lawson personally gave a donation (£20 this time). The re-pewing took more than 3 months; the seating was changed from the original enclosed seats to the open pews we now see. A reading desk, pulpit with stairs, an oak rail and turned balusters cost £18 10s. Gas lighting was provided in the pulpit and chancel, a stove was installed, and windows repaired.

To continue the practice of renting pews to families, card holders were ordered, cards printed, and pews were advertised for sale. The free pews were on a lower level in the middle section, and the rented pews were on a higher level on the north and south sides of the nave. You can still see card holders at the end of some pews today – they were not merely a device to reserve a place, but also an indication of a certain status. Contributions of £33 4s were also obtained for communion cloth, cushions and other furnishings, and the clock face was painted and gilded. In the following year the wood in the church was re-varnished. We are fortunate that during the church's history, so many people have made a commitment to keeping it in good condition.

By 1866 the burial ground again needed to be extended, to cope with the increasing population in the village. John Lawson gave more glebe land covering 1627 square yards, and covered the cost of draining the land, providing a wall and gate, and consecration fees – £63 19s 9d in total.

In these days, the church was almost always full, meaning around 500 people attended a service, invariably including a large number of visitors who stayed in the lodging houses. The organ and the choir were in the gallery, rather than in the chancel as they are today.

A little misunderstanding

The year 1866 provided an incident in Seaton Carew which made front page news, although for the wrong reasons. At the time, Irishmen were regarded with suspicion because a Fenian Society had been founded in America by Irishmen, with the aim of overthrowing British rule in Ireland, usually through stirring up trouble in areas of England which had Irish population.

A schooner 'Betsy Williams' had run aground at Seaton Snook and the timber cargo was cast adrift so she could be refloated. The owners employed a gang of 20 men, the majority being Irish, to recover the cargo using spiked poles and boathooks to secure the timber as it was washed up, and two of them were given boarding pikes. However, the cargo did not wash up at

Seaton so they ended up waiting on the beach for hours, getting quite wet and miserable.

Eventually they retired to the local public houses, and a group of them went to the Seaton Hotel. Talking to the barmaid while they thawed out, she asked what the strange items were that they had left in the passage. One joker told her these were pikes, and that they were Fenians who had come to invade Seaton. Unfortunately she took this seriously, warning the landlord, who alerted the village policeman to come and seize the weapons. Word soon spread in the village. A group of Seatonians grabbed sticks, stones, and bats, and challenged the Irishmen, forcing them to run off. Eventually the workers returned to the hotel, too cold to care what happened. They proved to be unarmed and honest citizens, so no further action was taken.

The story was somewhat exaggerated by the national press, which reported that fifty Irishmen had taken over the Seven Stars Hotel and, armed with pikes, were helping themselves from the casks in the cellar. The article claimed that the village PC had been called out and tried with several of the inhabitants to persuade them to leave, leading to a riot, with a couple of villagers being wounded. The police were said to have seized the pikes, formidable weapons 9 feet long, and it was claimed that the inhabitants of West Hartlepool were alarmed at having Fenians in their midst because nearly a third of the population was Irish! A correction had to be printed, noting that the locals were very anxious that the truth should be brought to light, especially the removal of the Fenian aspect of the story.

Treasure and temperance

In 1867 the villagers had a rare treat when a hoard of Spanish silver coins was uncovered in the sands following a heavy storm. Two men walking across the sands towards Port Clarence spotted a large amount of coins, which turned out to be Spanish dollars and doubloons. They stuffed their coats with the coins and went home to get their families, returning with buckets and whatever containers they could lay their hands on. By this time other villagers had found the treasure and they all worked until after dark, lighting fires on the beach to help them see. The Lord of the Manor was reported to be considering making a claim on all the treasure found, so the diggers had to secretly dispose of the coins in various ways, including selling them to collectors.

In the same year, a Temperance Hall opened in Ashburn Street, a brick building which cost £600, paid for by Edward Backhouse. The Deed of

Gift stipulated that the Trust would provide the Hall for events such as meetings, exhibitions, Bazaars, Soirees. But this had a particular purpose: the promotion or encouragement of Religion, Temperance, Literature, Science or Art, moral and intellectual improvement, "rational amusement of the public", and charitable purposes.

As the name of the Hall implies, the sale or consumption of any intoxicating drink was expressly prohibited. This came from a national campaign of the time, led by the Quakers, against the demon drink. Any lectures contrary to religion or morality were prohibited. It could not be used as a theatre, or for any purpose which might promote "Liquor traffic or Irreligion or Immorality". In later years concerts were held to raise money for good causes, films were shown, and scout troop meetings and country dance classes were held there.

Further developments

A major Seaton landmark was completed in 1869 – Staincliffe House, built as the home of Mr Thomas Walker, the owner of Walker's Sawmills in West Hartlepool, who employed 200 workers. He later became a Justice of the Peace. Initially the house was railed off almost to the cliff edge, with only a narrow path past the front of the house that carts and other vehicles could not use, but when Mr Walker's daughter was married, he opened the road in celebration. He also built six villas alongside, one of which gained notoriety in more recent times as the home of John Darwin, who staged his own disappearance in a canoe to enable his wife to make a fraudulent claim on his life insurance.

The Station Hotel was also built around this time, next to the railway station. A cottage next door was occupied by the station master.

Something happened in around 1873 which probably caused Mr Backhouse & his temperance supporters some displeasure: a small brewery was set up at Seaton Carew, run by Gilchrist and Ramsey. They had a horse and a large cart which took barrels of beer to Yarm and nearby towns, leaving at five in the morning. That must have woken up a few people in neighbouring houses.

The Post Office published a Directory in 1873 which showed a growing number of private residents compared to earlier publications. Professions now included a photographer, pilots (who guided ships in and out of the bay), a government school inspector, commercial travellers, a beer retailer and a worker at a manure works. The National School had Mr John Whincup as its Master and Miss Mary Woodward as its Mistress. As previously noted, a ladies' boarding school on The Green was run by Mrs Maria Cowper and her daughter Miss Mary Eliza Cowper.

Tudor Cottage, the house in the north west corner of The Green with a Swiss-style design, was owned by Robert Dixon, a magistrate. He was one of the villagers who had approved the proposal for the National School in 1844 and was a regular subscriber in support of its costs.

One of two lighthouses, the Seaton Low Light, was situated to the north of Staincliffe House, and was looked after by a man with a name that is not far off being very apt: Harry Burnicle. The High Light was the other lighthouse, now reconstructed on the Hartlepool Marina. The beach had about forty boats and cobles on it, indicating the importance of the sea to the working lives of the villagers. There were three sand dunes called Ladysmith, Mafeking and Spion Kop in front of the village, where bonfires were lit for celebration in the Boer War.

Around this time, Revd. John Lawson and the parishioners erected a gravestone with an anchor to the memory of unnamed sailors. The wording reads: *"Around this memorial stone lie the remains of sailors who perished in the mighty waters and whose bodies were washed on shore from wrecked vessels."* The west side reads *"The Lord knoweth them that are his"* and *"The sea gave up the dead which were in it"*. This stone was restored in 1898, although part of the anchor has since broken off.

Memorial to the unnamed sailors

There are 59 people buried in the churchyard who died through drowning. Some of them were washed up on the beach and others were taken from wrecked ships. They include three French sailors, three from a Russian barque and two German invaders from 1916. Not all those who drowned were unknown – some were identified through ship's records, presumably with the help of those who survived.

At each Remembrance Day and Sea Sunday, a short service of prayer is held at this memorial following our main communion service, to remember the sacrifices made by seafarers.

Vestry meeting records from 1875 show that Mr Mountjoy Pearse was the Vicar's Warden and Mr Swanson the People's Warden (succeeded by Mr Bakewell in 1879). Henry Lamb, a well-known local jeweller and clockmaker, was engaged to wind and maintain the church clock for £2 10s per annum. It was also necessary to employ an organ blower: J Odgers, who was succeeded by James Lithgo, the remuneration being around £1 a year. By 1884 Mr Pearse had moved to Stockton; Mr Bakewell became the Vicar's Warden and Mr Arthur Bunting (a local solicitor) the Parishioners' Warden.

The Local Board – grace and disgrace

A significant body which villagers had to engage with was the Seaton Carew Local Board, which was involved in agreeing changes to the local infrastructure of roads, fencing, and properties. The regional press reported their meetings, with some interesting news stories from around 1876-7 showing how the locals managed the village.

Revd. Lawson's involvement with the lifeboat caused him to ask the Board to improve the road along the sea front, as it was very difficult to get the lifeboat down to the sea for launching. However, the Board was reluctant to address this due to the cost. It was noted that when the lifeboat house had been built the previous year, it should have been located nearer the access point, hindsight being a wonderful thing.

The Seaton Carew churchwardens obviously thought the Board's reluctance to take action was unacceptable, and in support of their vicar, convened a meeting in the National School. This was very well attended by the local residents. Plans for a proposed diversion of the road were examined and it was unanimously agreed to carry out the alterations. These provided a clear road along the north end in case of shipwreck. Not for the first (or last) time, Seatonian people power won the day.

The predominance of farming at Seaton was illustrated when there was a debate at the Board over whether cows passing up and down the street were a nuisance or not and whether they should be prevented. One member thought it was a pleasant picturesque sight to see this, and that it *"bore testimony to the excellent quality of the Seaton milk"*. The Board was convinced and decided not to take any action.

This quaint picture soon changed. A series of incidents revealed personal animosity between some Board members. The story starts with George Taylor Vitty, a member of the Board and secretary to the Temperance Hall, and his mother, who owned the grocer's shop on the Front. Mrs Vitty wrote to ask the Board to remove a wooden structure they had placed between her private road and the sea, but they refused. She then caused annoyance by putting some information on the Board's expenses in her shop window. Clearly there was no such thing as a Freedom of Information request in those days and they seemed put out that their business details had been made publicly available.

Mr Vitty had also written to the Middlesbrough Gazette attacking the general policy of the Board. This did not go down well with the other members. At the Board's next meeting Mr Vitty's conduct was discussed in his presence and he became quite angry, shaking his fist in the Chairman's face. The Board requested Mr Vitty to stop supplying unfounded reports to the press. The motion having been passed, an outnumbered and indignant Mr Vitty disrupted the rest of the meeting by asking lots of questions and demanding immediate answers. The members lost patience and called a halt to the meeting.

Things quickly got worse after this. Two members of the Local Board, William Proctor (Board Surveyor) and Tobias Henry Tilly (a local solicitor and well-respected member of the congregation at Holy Trinity) were charged with assaulting George Vitty. A hearing took place at the West Hartlepool Borough Petty Sessions. The details of the case were that Mr Vitty had gone to the Board Room in Mr Proctor's Church Street home to examine the rate book, but was not permitted to see it until the Board meeting was over. When eventually allowed to examine the books, he reported that Mr Proctor had interrupted him, used bad language and threatened him. Then when Mr Vitty went to the window to call the police, Mr Proctor allegedly seized him by the shoulder and kicked him on his left thigh. The witnesses present, Mr Thomas Hudson and Mr Lithgo, testified that they did not see any assault, but the Bench found that the assault was committed and fined Mr Proctor 40 shillings plus costs, with an alternative of imprisonment for a month.

When Mr Tilly's part was considered in this case, Mr Vitty's legal representative admitted that the assault was not significant, so if an apology were tendered his client would let the matter drop. The newspaper report says "*The Bench, in the interests of the profession, said that would be the best course*". Given that Mr Tilly was a solicitor, this seems to be a case of looking after their own. But Mr Vitty was having none of this, and insisted that Mr Tilly had pushed him back against the passage wall, and "*whisked a notice across his face in a most insulting manner*". The Bench considered the case proved and imposed a penalty on Mr Tilly of 10 shillings plus costs. The incident does not seem to have marred the solicitor's reputation, so maybe we can draw our own conclusions from the affair.

CHAPTER 7 – JOHN LAWSON'S LATER YEARS

John Lawson's wife and companion Mary Lawson died in 1877 at the age of 75, and was buried in Holy Trinity churchyard. In the 1871 census five of the Lawsons' children were still living at the vicarage with them, and in the following census in 1881 the two unmarried daughters were still living there with their father.

The vicarage was a large property and the family employed a cook and housemaids – if John Lawson had not had a private income, the vicar's stipend would not have stretched to this. He is recorded as owning land in Yorkshire, ensuring that by making investments in assets he was not solely reliant on his family's fortune.

The following photograph of the vicarage dining room dates from between 1885 and 1890. It is possible that the paintings are of Lawson family members; perhaps they were borrowed from Boroughbridge Hall.

Vicarage dining room (by Revd. Pattison)

In the late 1800s, the village was lit by gas lights. One can imagine how dark it must have been before then, especially on a winter's evening when no moon was shining on the sea. In 1877 the Local Board dealt with a complaint that the lamplighter had been putting out the gas lights too early in the evening. Mr William Swanson (who was a churchwarden and a member of the Gas Committee) was asked to look into the matter. The Board believed that 10 pm on a Sunday was a reasonable time to extinguish the lights, but that during the week sufficient time should be allowed to let passengers arriving on the last train at 11 pm get into the village.

The following picture shows the wedding of Mr Swanson's daughter in 1890, taken outside the vicarage. This photograph, obtained from a parishioner, was taken by Revd. Pattison, who named the bride as Sarah Swanson. However, there is no trace of a Sarah Swanson in Holy Trinity's marriage registers. The Swanson wedding of 1890 was that of Emilie Willis Swanson, who married Charles Henry Stacey, a bank cashier from Sheffield. Revd. Pattison not only took the photograph but also officiated at the wedding.

Wedding of Miss Emilie Swanson and Mr Charles Stacey, 1890

In 1879 plans were put in place to build a road between Hartlepool and Seaton Carew. Prior to this, the village was completely separate from the town, apart from a small track. Two years later, plans were approved for tramlines to run between the Hartlepools (West Hartlepool and Old Hartlepool) and Seaton Carew. The trams became operational in 1901 and played a part in encouraging residential development in the village, as they provided a means for workers in the growing industries of West Hartlepool to travel to work from Seaton. They also brought an increase in day trippers from the town. The trams lasted until 1927, when they were replaced by trolley buses. Tickets for the tram journey were one penny per mile, apart from a special early morning rate of a halfpenny a mile for the workers.

Seaton Carew was annexed by West Hartlepool in 1882, which did not go down well with Seatonians. The locals liked their independence; this was a village where there was a gate at each end, one at the south end from the lifeboat house to the buoy house, and one at Staincliffe House to the north, and where everybody came out if a stranger came into the village! The annexing came at a cost, literally: the villagers were required to pay a rate of 10 old pence (now about 4p) in the pound to West Hartlepool, or else provide work in-kind, such as helping to construct the sea defences or shovel snow from the roads. Perhaps this should be adopted today as an alternative to paying your Council Tax.

Revd. Lawson's 50th anniversary in 1885 was recognised with a presentation of an illuminated address. This occasion does not seem to have been marked with as much ceremony as his 25th anniversary; however, John Lawson was now 78 years old and his health was starting to deteriorate, so perhaps it passed quietly. Around this time, assistance arrived in the form of a curate, Revd. James Whitehead Pattison, who had been ordained in 1882. There had been two previous curates, James Baynard (1875-6) and Frederick Robinson (1881-5). Revd. Lawson therefore managed for 40 years without a curate. By 1887, Revd. Pattinson was chairing the annual Vestry meeting, as John Lawson was not well enough to do so. The parish registers of this time reveal that other clergy assisted by conducting weddings, marriages and baptisms.

In around 1887 James Pattison took up photography, recording the everyday lives of Seaton's people, and producing some memorable images of Seaton Carew as well as other areas throughout the north east of England. Maureen Anderson's excellent book "Bygone Seaton Carew" contains many more of them. Revd. Pattison only stayed at Seaton for 5 years, moving to Bishop Auckland after John Lawson's death, having been appointed Rector of St John's Chapel. After Revd. Pattison's death in 1936 his daughter Catherine donated a selection of his photographs to the Bowes Museum.

By 1888 the church stonework could barely be seen for the ivy covering it, as the following photo from the Pattison collection shows.

An ivy-clad Holy Trinity in 1888

The tower has taller and more pointed pinnacles than those that can be seen today, and there is a cross at the apex of the east wall, which is now missing. The pinnacles were removed and capped in 1983 as they were in a dangerous condition. This photo also shows a gate in the east wall of the churchyard.

The original East window by William Wailes can be seen in the following picture of Holy Trinity, also taken by Revd. Pattison when the church was

Interior of Holy Trinity at Harvest 1888

decorated for Harvest Festival celebrations in 1888. As noted from the etching of the outside of the church, the earlier East window is much lower than today's window. The original pulpit can be seen on the right hand side of the church.

This photograph reveals that the north wall of the chancel (on the left) did not at that time hold the organ – it was still on the balcony. The gas light fittings can be seen on the wall, and the chancel is at a lower level than it is today.

A particularly interesting aspect of this photograph is that it reveals some features which must have been removed at a later date, certainly by 1890 judging by another similar Pattison image. An inscription runs up and down either side of the arch leading to the chancel. Although two words near the apex are not visible, we can assume that the full inscription reads: "Bless the Lord O my soul and all that is within me bless his holy name" and "Praise the Lord O my soul and forget not all his benefits". The beams in the chancel contain the words from an anthem by Maurice Green based loosely on Psalm 65, "Thou visitest the earth and blessest it/Thou crownest the year with thy goodness". There is also some lettering on the outer arch of the East window, but only the first word (While) and the last two (not cease) are visible on this image.

The John Lawson Lifeboat

The villagers' fondness for their vicar John Lawson, and their determination to do the right thing by him, was demonstrated clearly in the matter of the local lifeboat in 1888. The existing lifeboat, the Mary Isabella, was practically new, but the locals had expressed a lot of disappointment that this had not been named after Rev Lawson.

The local committee made a strong case, as for 50 years the vicar had been carrying out charitable work in the village and had been the secretary of the local branch of the Royal National Lifeboat Institution (RNLI) for most of this time. The RNLI gave in and agreed to let them have a new boat and name it the John Lawson. The Mary Isabella was moved to another station and the new boat arrived: another victory for the villagers.

On Saturday May 12th 1888 there was a parade of the new lifeboat, her crew, a brass band and the local committee. The vicar's daughter Miss Margaret Lawson christened the boat the John Lawson. It was launched in front of the village amid cheers, and then the crew, led by Mr Hood the coxswain, returned to be entertained at lunch by the committee at the Seven Stars Hotel.

The following photograph shows the horse drawn carriage on which the lifeboat was taken for launching.

The new lifeboat commissioned in 1888 – the John Lawson
Photograph by Revd. Pattison

John Lawson was a fervent supporter of the lifeboat at Seaton Carew, and worked very hard for it in a number of ways, including being Honorary Secretary of the local branch of the RNLI and keeping the accounts. He started a long lasting tradition: most of the vicars of Holy Trinity were appointed as Honorary Secretary. As long as his health allowed, he would turn up to cheer on the lifeboat crew whenever they were called out, even in the wildest of weather.

Death of Revd. Lawson

During the last four or five years of his life, poor health prevented Revd. Lawson from playing an active part in the parish, but he never lost interest in what was going on among his flock. After a lifetime dedicated to Holy Trinity and the parishioners of Seaton Carew, he passed away in 1890, aged 83. He was thought to have been the oldest clergyman in Durham Diocese at this time. The usual morning sermon was dispensed with at the church, and instead the Revd. Pattison gave a brief address on the saintly life and true Christian qualities of their departed vicar.

John Lawson's obituary published in the Northern Daily Mail gives an account of his dedication to the parish and his congregation:

"For 50 years he conducted the work of the parish alone, and he was never known to be absent from duty, not even for a holiday, for the whole of his vicariate. The generosity of the Revd. gentleman was equally noteworthy. Not only did he support the schools connected with the church, but he charged no burial fees. Apart from the exceptional interest evinced in church and parish affairs, the deceased was actively identified with the lifeboat work at Seaton, the lifeboat stationed there being named after him. He was invariably present when the boat was launched and despatched on its errands of mercy. Mr Lawson also took great interest in the Church Missionary Society, and, with the exception of Durham City, Seaton Carew contributed, for many years, larger sums than any parish in the county."

Although Revd. Lawson's health had been deteriorating over the last 4 years and his death would not have been a surprise, the villagers were distraught at the loss of their much-loved vicar and friend. Blinds were drawn throughout the village and other emblems of mourning displayed. The funeral service and graveside

John Lawson's grave in Holy Trinity churchyard by Revd. Pattison

rites were attended by many clergy, the family and local dignitaries as well as the villagers whom Revd. Lawson had made it his life's work to help. A photograph taken by Revd. Pattison shows the amount of floral tributes that were left at his graveside after the tombstone had been erected.

A letter was published from an unknown gentleman in the Northern Daily Mail two days after John Lawson's funeral, which showed a great affection for this clergyman and gives a very personal account of his qualities:

"Sirs – I am a non-conformist but I have often listened to the late Vicar of Seaton Carew, and his preaching always made a deep impression on me. His sermons were read; but there was a sweetness of tone, a gentleness of manner, and a keen intellectual force about the effort that acted like a charm on his listeners. I shall never forget him, and if his influence for

good has been equal to others as in me, he has done well indeed. I have an old picture of him in the prime of life – long before I knew him – and there is a nobility of gentleness in his smiling face that is particularly attractive.

…Perhaps at no time did his influence and goodness appear so vast as at a death bed. Then he seemed transfigured, his face shone in his fervour, and he seemed to lift his soul away above mundane things. Especially tender was he in one such scene. A member of one of the oldest village families – a man stricken in years, whose life, if rough, had been pure, and for whom the late vicar entertained great affection – lay dying. In spite of growing infirmities, and doctors' injunctions, the dear old man, evading the gentle vigilance of his family, made his way to the death bed. He needed to be helped up the stairs so weak in body was he, but once before the dying one, he seemed to renew his strength. Raising his bent body straight, and lifting his aged hand towards heaven, he stood upright for twenty minutes, praying and comforting his humble friend. It would require a greater pen than mine to portray the intense earnestness of the man, the gentleness of his manner, the sweetness of his counsel, and the loving tenderness of his voice."

John Lawson memorial window

It was inevitable that the parishioners would want to remember Revd. Lawson after his death, and a beautiful memorial window was installed in the South side of the nave. This is shown on page 87.

The inscription on a brass plate at the foot of the window reads:

"I am the Good Shepherd"
To the glory of God and in memory of the Revd. John Lawson MA
for 55 years Vicar of this Parish who died 10th August 1890.
This window is erected by Parishioners and Friends.

This window is believed to be by Clayton & Bell of London, who established the most consistently productive and influential of all the Victorian stained glass studios and trained a vast number of artists and craftsmen. Christ is shown in two poses as the Good Shepherd: in the upper section he carries a lamb on his shoulders and holds a crook, and in the lower section he is seated among his flock. The window contains the opening line of Psalm 23, The Lord is my Shepherd. This is particularly fitting for one who guided the flock of Seaton Carew in faithfulness over so many years.

CHAPTER 8 – FAMILY MEMORIALS FROM JOHN LAWSON'S ERA

There are several family memorials in the church which date from the time of John Lawson. He evidently encouraged this as a means of remembering loved ones.

Anna and Jane Wray

The earliest stained glass window still surviving in Holy Trinity Church is in memory of Anna and Jane Wray and is shown on page 88. The inscription reads:

Anna Wray died ye 9th of Dec A.D. 1843

Jane Wray died ye 12th of May A.D. 1856

Anna and Jane's father was a doctor, George Wray from Stockton, and their mother was Jane (née Catterick). Their grandfather Christopher Wray was a surgeon, who married Anna Maria Ferrand, of the Ferrand family of Harden Grange, Bingley in Yorkshire. Anna Maria's father Richardson Ferrand (1723-1769) served as Mayor of Stockton in the years 1751 and 1762.

Anna Wray died in Stockton, in 1843, but there is no reference to her life in any official records.

The 1851 census at Seaton Carew records a Jane Wray (born in Glasgow in 1808), who was unmarried and a landed proprietor, employing a live-in cook and housemaid. She owned land in Dovecot Street in Stockton. In 1851 Jane was named as one of the subscribers to the carpet exhibited by Queen Victoria at the Great Exhibition at the Crystal Palace. Jane died in Stockton in 1856.

This window has elements of the grisaille style adopted in the original East window. In terms of colour and design, Neil Moat of Newcastle University believes it could have been G J Baguley of Newcastle, but some aspects of the upper coat of arms are of a higher standard and the lettering is not characteristic of this artist. It may therefore be by Henry Mark Barnett (1832-88, established c.1858) who was one of Wailes' Newcastle-based pupils.

The arms depicted in the window are those of the Wray and Ferrand families, commemorating the marriage of Christopher Wray and Anna Maria Ferrand. The birds in the Wray window are martlets, a common item in heraldry. There are some inaccuracies in the colouring and shape of the Ferrand arms compared to the authentic version.

The Fawcus family

The Fawcus family were a notable family in Seaton during the 1850s to 1870s. The head of the family, Robert, was a businessman and he and his wife Anna Maria had a large family. Their faith was very important to them. A lot of information has been passed down the generations of their family; thanks to their generosity, we have a very full picture of the lives of Robert, Anna Maria and their children.

The centre window in the south wall of the nave is a memorial to Anna Maria Fawcus, shown **on** page 89. The inscription reads:

In memory of Anna Maria wife of Robert Fawcus Esq.
died May 15ᵗʰ 1871 aged 50

This window is by Messrs G J Baguley of Newcastle, already mentioned in connection with the Wray window. George Joseph Baguley (1834-1915) was a former pupil of William Wailes, establishing his own studio in around 1867.

The central image in the window shows Mary washing Christ's feet. The lower part shows Jesus being taken down from the Cross in preparation for burial, with the marks of the nails clearly visible in his feet and hands. The upper image is of the Ascension. The painting is very detailed in places, such as the bowl of fruit on the table and the pattern in the carpeting.

Robert Fawcus was born in 1817 in Stepney, Middlesex to parents Robert Fawcus and Ann (née Evans). Tragedy struck while he was still a baby, when his father died in 1818. His mother Ann then married her brother-in-law Henry. This meant that Robert's uncle became his step-father as well.

Marrying your brother's widow was illegal at this time. To get round this, the couple declared on their marriage licence application that there was no impediment, despite knowing this was untrue. To avoid detection they married well outside of the area at St Dunstan's Church, Stepney in Middlesex. Their wedding took place only three days after applying; the reason became apparent six months later when their first son was born. Ann and Henry went on to have a large family, and Robert and his elder brother John ended up with 9 step-brothers and sisters by 1839.

Robert's wife Anna Maria was born in 1820 in Kingston, Surrey, to Thomas and Deborah Speciall, who were Quakers. Robert and Anna Maria married in Holy Trinity Church, Stockton in 1841.

When still relatively young, Robert went into business with his step-father, as Henry Fawcus and son, Timber Merchants and Ship owners, based at Stockton and Middlesbrough. Robert seems to have been responsible for the company's foreign connections, and he and Anna Maria spent their honeymoon in Hamburg. However, by 1842 the company had gone bankrupt and their Stockton properties were auctioned off.

Robert then moved to Hartlepool, working in the coal industry. He took advantage of the developments in railways and shipping to find a new career as an agent for collieries, finding markets for the coal and arranging transportation. He worked at Byers Green collieries in County Durham until 1851 and must have been more successful in this line of work; Anna Maria's mother Deborah wrote in her diary that when she visited, Anna Maria drove her and her other daughters on visits and picnics in her gig.

When Robert left Byers Green, the agents and workmen there presented him with an elegant inscribed tea service, expressing their high regard for him and regret at his departure. By 1851 the family were in a pleasant house in Seaton Carew, and Robert had an office in West Hartlepool.

The Fawcus house in Seaton Carew was on The Green to the west of North Road, on the left hand side of the pair shown in the photograph (right). This was later combined with the adjoining house and became the Haraap & Sterndale girls' school. A letter from an unknown

Fawcus family house on The Green

gentleman dated 1873 states that the Fawcus house "while very pretty at the front, is unbelievably beautiful at the back, being contained under glass and boasting every type of flower, fruit and tree." It is said that all the wooden panelling and other items in the house were from ships.

The couple had a large family – 10 sons and 4 daughters. Although this house was larger than many in Seaton, it must have still been a little cramped when everyone was at home, especially if the younger children were being boisterous, but discipline would have been important in this family. Their religious beliefs were very important to them; Robert led family prayers every morning and his sons read the lessons. Twelve of the children are shown in this very early photograph of the family:

Robert, Anna Maria and Fawcus family c1860

The children were Henry (born 1842), Thomas Powell (1843), Robert Speciall (1845), Arthur (1847), John (1848), Anna Maria (1851), William Albert (1851), Emily Josephine (1853), Evans (1855), Charles Octavius (1856), Frances Mary (1857), Ernest Augustus (1859), Lucy Beatrice Evelyn (1861), and Louis Edward (1864).

The eldest, Henry, had a tragic life; he lost his first wife and three infant sons, all of whom are buried in Holy Trinity churchyard. He committed suicide in 1903 by shooting himself, distressed at his business being in difficulties. His brother Evans had worked for him for about 30 years so became unemployed after this sad event.

John (known as Jack) showed great kindness to the rest of his family when they needed assistance. He paid for his niece to stay at university when his brother Evans lost his job, and employed a live-in nurse to look after his elder brother Robert who became an invalid.

Frances Mary married James Wilcocks Carrall in 1878. Jim worked in the Customs Service in China. Further information on Frances' life is included later.

Ernest died on Boxing Day in Cheshire aged only 26, in an explosion on a ship he was inspecting. It appears from the inquest report that he was still celebrating Christmas when he was called out, and did not put out his cigar.

Two of the Fawcus offspring married relatives. Anna married Henry Evans Fawcus, who was a distant cousin. William married Ada Fawcus who was born in Denmark, his grandfather Henry's daughter from his first marriage.

Robert spent so much time on business in Hamburg that he decided to take German citizenship in 1854. Anna Maria must have accompanied him on a trip in January 1856, as their son Charles Octavius was born there.

A descendant of Robert Fawcus, Dr Mary Tiffen, has kindly provided a transcript of some very personal letters written by Robert and Anna Maria. Mary is the granddaughter of Frances Fawcus, Robert's eleventh child. These provide a fascinating insight into the relationship between the husband and wife during their separation due to Robert's business travels. Anna Maria had support from household servants (a cook and a nurse), but she was clearly devoted to her children and closely involved in their upbringing and education.

A letter by Robert to his parents describes the death of Anna Maria's mother Deborah Speciall in 1855 in a way that demonstrates the importance of the family's faith:

"My dearest Father and Mother,

I write to inform you that my poor mother-in-law died this morning at quarter to 11 – and truly her end was pious and we may all earnestly wish that our latter end may be like hers. All her family were around her and during her freedom from pain up to the last she expressed her affection for them, and her desire to depart – almost her last connected words if not her very last were "Bless the Lord oh my soul, blessed be his name for ever". But seldom does it fall to the lot of anyone to see many good Christians depart, but the sight of even one dying so patient, and full of faith and hope and so fearless to cross death's cold stream is sufficient to cause even in a worldly breast, the feeling that a long life well spent in the service of our maker and our God, ensures a reward in his presence at the moment of dissolution. Already her spirit is with him who has sustained her and doubtless if permitted to disembodied spirits to look down upon their earthly associates hers will frequently linger around this place. May it be your lot, and may it be mine and Maria's also, when our career is finishing, to be surrounded by all the dearest survivors of our families and to perceive a kind affectionate feeling amongst them."

In 1856 Robert went on a business trip to Hamburg, Cologne, St Petersburg, and Copenhagen. The Treaty of Paris, ending the Crimean War with Russia, had been signed in March that year and it was likely that Robert was trying to restore business links. The expansion of West Hartlepool as a port provided good opportunities for merchants of coal or timber, and ship brokers, such as the Fawcus family.

The letters Anna Maria wrote to Robert while he was on his business trip with Mr Pease show her strong faith. She urged Robert to read a psalm every day, as she intended to do while he was away. She asked him to consider bringing up their second son Tom to become a minister, as with so many sons she thought they should dedicate one, hoping it would bring a blessing on them. What Tom thought about this is not recorded, but we can draw our own conclusions, as his choice of career was not the ministry; he followed in his father's footsteps and became a timber merchant.

Anna Maria's letters demonstrate that she and Robert were very close and showed great affection towards each other; she repeatedly tells him how much his letters mean and that she is missing him. After nearly 3 weeks of being apart, she wrote *"You say I must tell you all my thoughts, they may be expressed in a very short word 'you'. When the children are gone to bed I sit and think about you and every morning we have a walk directly after breakfast towards Hartlepool, and as they play about, I walk on thinking about you and recalling the many times we have trod those sands together, and longing for the time when we shall do so again… I really shall be too happy when I get you back, tho' mind I don't believe that you will be half as good as you promise. It is very easy to promise when you have not my provoking self to annoy you."*

The letters also show how hectic it was with such a large family, especially at times when she had to change some of the servants. She comments *"You say that you fancy me on the receipt of this harassed with my new servants, it is quite the reverse, <u>they</u> have not begun to harass me yet, tho' the old ones did till <u>almost the last</u> and then went away, weeping, cook most violently. I have been very poorly and obliged to have Mr Longbotham. When he called on Tuesday*

I said 'What shall I do, my servants all leave today and I have no one to sleep in the house'. He was very compassionate and promised to send me some one from Greatham and accordingly, just as the girls were leaving the house, a nice comfortable old fashioned woman arrived named Bessie."

Anna Maria recorded that she attended church while Robert was away, and other members of the congregation showed concern for her during her husband's absence and asked after him. She provided the celebration cake for Revd. Lawson's silver anniversary tea party.

At some stage after 1864 the Fawcus family moved to Over Dinsdale Hall, near Middleton One Row, a mansion with stables, extensive grounds down to the banks of the river Tees, a salmon fishery, woodland and farms. However, they did not live there for long: in 1870, Robert Fawcus put Over Dinsdale up for sale. While it was on the market, Anna died, on 15th May 1871. Robert commissioned the stained glass window on the south side of Holy Trinity Church, Seaton Carew, in her memory.

In the 1881 census Robert was a retired Coal Merchant, residing in London. He had moved to a house in Norbiton, near Kingston-on-Thames, Surrey, to be near his sons working in London. He named this residence Over Dinsdale in fond memory of his happy family home in the north. He died there in 1894 aged 78, after a 3-day illness.

The Fawcus family were keen supporters of the church and the school, being named in subscription lists whenever Revd. Lawson made an appeal.

Dr Mary Tiffen has published a book, "Friends of Sir Robert Hart – Three Generations of Carrall Women in China", which details the adventures of Robert and Maria's daughter Frances and her husband James Wilcocks Carrall in 19th century expatriate China. Frances' older brothers Arthur and Jack were friends of Jim's and visited him in London, later introducing Frances to him. Frances and Jim married in 1878 and left for China soon afterwards, as he had obtained a Customs post in China as a result of his mother meeting Sir Robert Hart, Inspector-General of the Chinese Imperial Customs. Jim later became Hart's Private Secretary.

Frances and Jim had 10 children (continuing the Fawcus tradition of a large family), but their first, Edward, died only a few days after his premature birth in 1878. There followed five girls up to 1884: Emily, Muriel, Maude, Kathleen and Frances junior, then a much longed-for boy Eric, girls Gwen and Phyllis, and finally James in 1900 when Frances was 43. Sir Robert Hart became a friend and was godfather to some of the children, continuing in correspondence with them for years afterwards. He described Frances as soft, unaffected, good natured and not exacting, but was not quite as complimentary about her husband Jim.

During her time in China, Frances not only ran the household and nursed the family through the illnesses which were prevalent, but also entertained in support of her husband's role. She showed courage when China was subjected to attack by France in 1884. She did not flee their home in Foochow, although many wealthy Chinese were moving out and conditions were difficult, including a shortage of rice. The family had a lengthy leave in 1887-9 which they spent in England at the family home in Kingston-on-Thames. This period was the last time Frances saw her father Robert Fawcus before his death in 1894.

The year 1902 brought tragedy for Frances. Most of the family contracted scarlet fever, and firstly her husband Jim then her youngest daughter Phyllis died. Frances decided to leave China and return to England. Her brothers Arthur and Jack were executors of Jim's will, and took the family to Kingston-on Thames. Frances and her children were amazed at the number of new Fawcus relatives that they encountered, and although the welcome was warm, they found the weather very cold compared to China. The year ended with another disaster when Frances junior died of appendicitis.

Frances and Jack provided a home at Over Dinsdale in Kingston to any family member who needed it. Frances died in 1929.

The Lithgo family

The Lithgos are one of the oldest families in Seaton Carew and have had an involvement with Holy Trinity across many generations. The earliest Seatonians are shown below. The first James Lithgo shown here had a father George, born in Greatham.

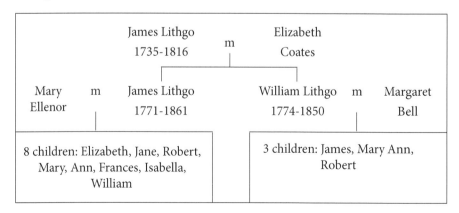

The Tees Pilot Lithgos described in this book are mainly descended from William and Margaret's son James. James married Jane Welsh and had a large family of four girls and three boys. Their sons included John Lithgo, who married Jessie Scott and had nine children: James born 1867, John (1869-1872), William Scott (1871), twins Jessie and Christina (1873), Jane (1876), Fanny(1877), Mary (1879) and John (1884).

A large copy of the King James Bible was donated to Holy Trinity by the Lithgo family, with the following inscription:

To the Glory of God
and in memory of William Scott Lithgo
born 1871, died April 29th 1960
and his wife Hannah Lithgo
died January 16th 1941

William Scott Lithgo is regarded as a central character among the Lithgo family and in later years was referred to as "Grandad" by many of the villagers. He is shown on the front row of the following photograph with his family.

Back row L to R: James Edward, John senior, Fanny Stewart, Mary Elizabeth (Netta) , John

Front row L to R: Jessie (twin sister of Christina), Jane, Jessie Scott, William Scott, Christina (Tinny) (twin sister of Jessie)

From their earliest days in the 1700s, this family had a strong association with the sea. Many of them were Tees pilots, skilled sailors who guided ships in and out of the harbour.

William Scott Lithgo wrote a diary and a record of Seaton Carew in the 1870s and 80s, both of which provide a detailed picture of the daily lives of the villagers. He started earning money at an early age, operating the blower for the church organ at an annual salary of £1 5s. The organist was Miss Lawson, the vicar's daughter. In Revd. John Lawson's day there were three services on a Sunday, and the four groups of the choir (men, ladies, girls and boys) each had a separate practice during the week. William also worked at weddings and funerals.

The enterprising Master Lithgo had several other jobs: delivering milk which paid a shilling a week, assisting the postman, and carrying meat orders to customers for the local butcher. As if that was not enough, he helped the Lithgo family run their bath house by bringing pails of sea-water for the visitors to use. He went out on fishing expeditions with his father where he helped to put bait on the lines, remove the fish and carry it home when they got back on land, receiving three pence for this. He put some of his earnings into a club for his mother at Mrs Vitty's shop; he noted in his diary that the shop had groceries on one side and drapery on the other.

William recalls that Mr Bakewell, a grain merchant who owned warehouses at the docks, used to bring a big sack of wheat to Seaton at Christmas, and allowed the villagers to come with cans to collect portions of it. They made it into a traditional dish dating from medieval times: frumenty, a thick wheat porridge, which was eaten on Christmas Eve.

According to William, in the 1880s the village had its own coat of arms, showing a sea coal rake. Farmers brought their carts to collect the sea coal, selling it for a shilling a load. In those days working people could not afford coal from the mines; they took the opportunities that nature provided on the beach. Villagers paid ten shillings to have a row of potato plants ploughed out at Hunter House Farm and they gathered the potatoes to take home, which lasted them the winter. Many people also kept a pig.

In the winter, boards were put up along The Front to keep the sand out, and in summer these were taken down and laid out to form a footpath over the sands. The youngsters of the village had another use for them however; they made rafts out of them and used a broom shank to propel them through the pools of water that were left when the tide went out.

The voices of children are often missing from historical accounts, but William looked back fondly on his childhood experience of church and school:

> *"The peaceful Sundays are something to remember; the gentlemen with their silk hats coming to church with their wives and families; the choir stalls were family pews and so were nearly all the pews on both sides. The organ and choir were upstairs. We only had one school for both boys and girls, and we went from Sunday School to Church with our teachers.*
>
> *What a great event our Sunday School Christmas party was, when the Vicar, Mr John Lawson sat at the desk and our teachers and pupils had to go and stand whilst he heard our teachers give an account of our attendance and character. Then we got a book, and after our tea we got a Yule cake and an orange and apple to bring home.*
>
> *In those days at funerals the bearers had silk hats which they got from the big houses. When there were weddings all the village was decorated with flags, and so were all the boats and cobles on the beach. Minstrels used to go round on Christmas Eve and New Year's Eve with white shirts and faces blacked with burnt cork and wearing old silk hats which they got from the big houses. They had a tambourine, bones, and a tin whistle or flute."*

About five families of Quakers came every summer, and entertained the villagers by setting off big balloons every night and providing a good firework display. William remembers a Captain Russell visiting each summer and putting up a big telescope for the villagers to look through. There were only two houses on the cliff south of Staincliffe House at this time, owned by Mr Kitty Thompson and Mr Bunting.

There was a lot of fishing activity in the 1880s, not only by locals but also from far and wide. Vessels came from the Thames to catch the whiting, and large fishing cobles came from around the north coast ports to collect mussels for bait. If the weather was bad they moored up and slept in the Lifeboat Watch House and the Temperance Hall.

When the lifeboat needed to be launched, it took eight horses to pull it, and someone had to go to Hunter House farm to borrow them. If some of the crew were unavailable, any strong and fit men would volunteer to go out on the lifeboat.

The caring nature of the villagers was demonstrated by William's aunt, who retained a big chest of dry clothes which were kept clean and mended in case they were needed for crews who were rescued from wrecked ships. Other sources report that when unknown seamen were buried at Holy Trinity, very often the villagers would provide wreaths, or attend the funeral when otherwise no-one would be present. This was a community that took seriously its responsibilities for helping others and showed common human kindness.

William and his father John went salmon fishing with nets to provide fish for the shop on The Front owned by Ambrose Storer. William's mother, Jessie Scott Lithgo, baked bread and teacakes and he used to go round the houses and farms in Seaton selling them.

Life was hard for those who relied on the sea for their living. There seems to have been a lot of competition for the pilots to be assigned boats to bring in and take out. William records several occasions when the weather was rough and boats were nearly lost. One incident in 1888 was particularly difficult. He went with his father to bring a ship out, and saw the brig Granite coming in from Redcar. The ship struck the North Gare in a gale. The lifeboat was launched; most of the crew were away so they had to round up as many men as were willing to help. They got close to the ship but made a bad shot with the grappling hook, and it fell on the rail and slipped overboard. They could not get back again because the inexperienced crew could not row effectively. Although the Middlesbrough lifeboat set off to help, it could not reach the Granite in time and she broke up; all the ship's crew drowned. This must have been a traumatic experience for those who witnessed it.

In 1889 William worked as a fisherman with Ambrose Storer, with two fleets of nets, a coble on the beach and a coble at Snook End. Despite working night and day the fishing was not very good, and William earned only £20 for the whole season. The following year was just as bad. The locals must have developed good judgement to know when it was safe to go out on the sea.

The villagers amused themselves by organising sailing regattas and competitions such as tug-of-war. Colonel Thomlinson brought metal carriers from the blast furnace and challenged the winners to pull them for a prize of ten shillings. William's team managed it; he proudly notes that they won the tug-of-war every year until the Armistice.

William married Hannah Evans in 1895 and initially rented rooms from Ambrose Storer for 5 shillings a week. He must have found it difficult to get up in the morning, as he remembered a wire led from the back door through the bedroom window with a bell to call him up. They then moved to a house in Charles Street for £8 a year.

Some Seaton families had Tees Pilots across several generations: Hood, Bulmer, Lister, Fryett, Snowden, Hunter, Pounder and Hodgson. Some of them also served as volunteers in the lifeboat crew, and are shown in the photograph overleaf with the Francis Whitbourn lifeboat, circa 1908.

L to R: Wm Lithgo, A Anderson, E Corner, T Hodgson, J Bulmer, Geo Hodgson, A N Bunting, J Noddings, H Wake, R Greig, Geo Storrer (second cox), J Elliott, J Lithgo (cox)

Ralph Thompson Walker

Ralph Thompson Walker was born in 1849 at Middleton Grange to Ralph Walker and Ann (neé Corker). He was a farmer at Fence House Farm in Greatham, which was about 20 minutes' walk from Greatham station. Ralph married Mary Stephenson in Warden, Northumberland in 1872. He was an officer of the 4th Durham Artillery Volunteers, with the rank of Sub-Lieutenant.

He died on 12th September 1876 at Helmsley, aged only 27, and is buried at Holy Trinity. The Northern Echo reported that he was visiting his father-in-law Marshall Stephenson when he fell ill and died: the cause was epilepsy. Ralph was described as a keen sportsman, a genial neighbour and a kind friend.

After his death, Ralph Walker's farm stock, tools and machinery were put up for sale, including horses, sheep, pigs and poultry.

A window was commissioned in 1878 by Mary Walker in memory of her late husband. The inscription reads:

"Suffer the little children to come unto me"
To the glory of God and in memory of Ralph Thompson Walker who died 12th
September 1876. This window is erected by his widow.

The design represents the story, recorded in several gospels, of Jesus telling the disciples to let children approach him. There is also a personification of Faith.

This window, shown on page 90, was designed by G J Baguley (as for the Fawcus window). Mr Baguley's letter asking the vicar to approve the design stated that the window would be made so as to obstruct the light as little as possible. The upper and lower parts of the window achieve this, with less density of colour than other windows.

CHAPTER 9 – A NEW ERA BEGINS

Reverend Francis Warren Parry Jones Mortimer Vicar 1890 – 1894

Francis Mortimer was born in 1863 at Walthamstow. He was educated at Eton College and Corpus Christi College Cambridge, gaining his B.A. degree in 1885 and his M.A. in 1889. He was ordained Deacon at Chester and served briefly at Birkenhead before being ordained Priest at Durham Cathedral in 1886. His first post was as a curate, serving with his father at the Parish of St. Mary the Virgin, Norton on Tees. He married Catherine Rose Levett in 1887 in Rugby and they had three children: Reginald, Francis and Eleanor.

Revd. Mortimer

In 1890 he became vicar of Holy Trinity. There must have been quite a contrast for parishioners between the long-serving John Lawson and the 27 year old Francis Mortimer, and events showed that the new vicar certainly had plenty of energy. One of his earliest tasks was a restoration project in 1891.

The Diocese required permission to be sought for alterations to its churches, known as a faculty. This is still the case. The faculty record is kept in Durham University Library, and outlines the extent of the work being proposed:

> *"That in consequence of the bad state of repair of the present floor of the Church and the defective nature of the present heating apparatus and of the present organ being worn out, it is proposed to build an organ chamber on the north side of the Chancel and erect a new organ in it. To build a heating chamber on the north side of the Chancel and erect a new heating apparatus therein. To build a new vestry also on the north side of the said chancel. To lay down a new floor in the Church and Chancel and to make a step at the entrance to the Chancel."*

This work established most of the internal structure of the church as we know it today. The organ replaced the one in the gallery. From other records we know that the chancel was raised about a foot to its current position, and its floor was re-laid with a tessellated pavement (one made up of small tiles). The whole project was estimated to cost £689.

Durham University Library holds a plan for the alterations, which shows two possible designs for the new vestry. One was almost like a conservatory in its shape, with five sides projecting from the north wall. However, it was the more traditional square shape which was built. The plans, drawn by the architect H Weatherill from Stockton, confirm that at that time the pulpit, which at that time was made of wood, was situated on the south side of the church rather than its current position on the north side, as we have already noted in the photograph of the interior from 1888.

A later faculty refers to tablets of the Creed, the Lord's Prayer and the Ten Commandments. These can also be seen on the previous picture of the church in 1888, on page 52 which clearly shows two of them on the east wall of the nave, at either side of the opening to the chancel. They appear to be in marble.

A dedication service was held on October 11th 1891, at which special sermons were preached in both the morning and evening to crowded congregations. This was the first time that a surpliced choir sang in the church. Just in case parishioners thought that the work was completed and no further demands would be made on their pockets, collections were taken in aid of the restoration fund, raising 10 guineas. This was classed as an informal reopening in the press report; it was noted that the church would be formally reopened with special preachers when the new organ was ready.

The 10 years before Rev Mortimer arrived saw an unprecedented increase in population in Seaton Carew, from 925 in 1881 to 2147 in 1891. There were now more than six times as many people in the parish as when Holy Trinity first opened.

In 1895 the organ was further improved by painting and decorating the organ pipes and the case. The design was completed by Dr Knowles, of York Mediaeval Art Works.

Seaton Snook

Just two years into Revd. Mortimer's incumbency, a controversial issue arose which could have had a detrimental effect on the church and the village. A proposal was made by the Tees Port Sanitary Authority to establish a hospital for cholera patients by converting cottages at Seaton Snook (the south end of the village). While cholera epidemics were not unusual around this time, such a proposal indicates that this one must have caused quite an emergency.

There was a huge outcry at the idea of setting up a hospital in Seaton, because those who died would have to be buried in Holy Trinity's churchyard and it would destroy the long-standing image of the village as a high quality watering place. In addition the proposal had been made without the consent of the Local Board, which had sanitary control of the area. The opposition was well organised, with a petition from local residents adding to the weight of the Board's discussions. An interesting alternative suggestion was made, that the Tees authority should set up a floating hospital.

Fortunately the Seaton Snook proposal died a death (people power winning the day once more), and in 1895 the Tees Floating Hospital was indeed established, to nurse ships' crew members who carried infections or contagious disease. This was moored at Seal Sands and contained two wards, an administration block, a laundry and a mortuary.

In the late 19th century there was an annual military camp set up at Seaton Snooks for various detachments including the Durham Light Infantry and the Northumberland Fusiliers. This very exposed area right at the edge of the sea was subject to extreme cold and wind, but one report notes there were few complaints about the raw atmosphere. The camp rose at 5 am and Holy Trinity Church was opened early for a 7 am Holy Communion service. At 10.30 the brigade paraded in review order for divine service on an open space at the south end of the Snook. They had their own clergy, who led a service at the local Anglican church wherever they were based, in this case Holy Trinity, but the Catholics among the camp had to march to St Joseph's in the centre of Hartlepool for their service.

Good works and social activities

A statistical return for 1891-2 which had to be submitted to the Diocese records that the church had 200 sittings for which pew rents were charged, and 306 free seats. A decision had recently been taken to open the church daily for prayer, making it more accessible for the people of Seaton Carew.

By this time there were 131 children on roll at the school. The Sunday Schools were also very healthy in number, with infant and junior sections totalling 157 children, although the attendance had not improved much since

Revd. Lawson's day – it hovered around the 100 mark. There were plenty of volunteers for the Sunday school – 3 men and 11 women were teachers there.

There was also a Bible Class for adults, which around 27 people attended. A group of 12 lay district visitors assisted the vicar; the congregation made contributions to cover their salaries and also those of the organist, choir and clerk as well as the heating and lighting. There was a large choir, consisting of 36 men and 9 ladies, begging the question as to how they all fitted into the chancel. The previous photograph from 1888 shows that the choir stalls in place at that time extended further forward than the current ones, but they must still have been uncomfortably full with this number of choristers.

In 1892 a Hartlepool branch of the Girls' Friendly Society was started, with representation in Seaton Carew, encouraged by Mrs Mortimer. This organisation was first founded in 1875 by the national Church of England and quickly became an international movement, devoted to the expansion of women's self-respect. The Society's founder Mrs Mary Townsend was very concerned about the vast number of girls in domestic service, who were often exploited through very long working hours and few days off. The society's aim was to help young women to help themselves, by giving them opportunities to develop their potential and pursue their aspirations, so they could grow in confidence and value themselves and others equally. There were several well-to-do families in Seaton Carew with servants, as evidenced in census returns; one wonders how they reacted to this new movement.

Mrs Mortimer began a village tradition which was to flourish and grow for 60 years. Under the GFS banner, informal support that was going on within a community became more organised and sustained.

The Mothers' Union was another tradition which was well supported, with monthly meetings in the church hall. Each meeting began with a prayer and ended with a blessing, and in between a visiting speaker would inform and entertain the gathering. It was also a social occasion, and despite the title it seems it was not necessary to be a mother in order to join the branch.

But good works were also part of the Mothers' Union activity, with support for particular organisations, such as the Waifs and Strays Society, the Lifeboat Association and the Mission to Seamen. While the number of barefoot ragamuffins present on the village streets was probably quite low (although not totally eradicated), the ladies of the Mothers' Union would have felt a strong affinity with the two sea-faring charities. Many of them had husbands, fathers, brothers and sons who risked their lives saving others or carrying out their business on the sea. As we have seen, deaths of known and unknown persons washed up on the beach or taken off wrecks were also a constant reminder of the power of the sea. The Church Missionary Society and the Church Army were also well supported.

Members of the Mothers' Union also made a significant contribution to the running expenses of the church with their craft skills. Sewing, handicrafts and baking were all evident on the stalls at the sales of work and garden parties held to raise funds, and these efforts made a huge contribution to the life of the church and ensured it could be maintained in good condition.

It was not only Mothers' Union members who showed generosity towards good causes. The members of Holy Trinity Church continued to make donations to charitable organisations. As with the Mothers' Union, some of their choices give a clear indication of their concern for those who made a living at sea, such as the Mission to Seamen and the Port of Hull Society for the Religious Instruction of Sailors. Hartlepool Hospital and the Church Missionary Society (CMS) also benefited. The Port of Hull Society was set up by William Dykes, who was a shipbuilder from Hull and whose son John Baccus Dykes composed many Victorian hymns including Eternal Father Strong to Save, Holy Holy Holy, and Nearer My God to Thee (reputed to have been played as the Titanic sank).

Service with a smile

The inhabitants of Staincliffe House had an interesting brush with a celebrity in 1893. John Lawrence Toole (1830-1906) was a comic actor and theatrical producer. He was famous for his roles in farce and melodramas and was the first actor to have a West End theatre named after him. He was appearing at West Hartlepool in a show and was out for a walk on the beach at Seaton Carew when it became foggy and he lost his way. Seeing lights on in Staincliffe House and thinking it was a hotel, he walked in, sat down and asked a member of the household staff for a brandy and soda. She was taken aback but brought him a drink and it was only when he tried to pay and she refused that he realised his mistake. The Walker family were most amused and invited Mr Toole to stay for dinner, then drove him to the theatre in the family carriage for his evening performance.

The prophetic element of this story came with the newspaper report that claimed the house was going to become a hotel, with plans to call it "Toole's Hotel". While that name was not adopted, Staincliffe House certainly did open

Staincliffe House, with Seaton Low Light
in the distance
By Revd. Pattison

as a hotel, although not until the late 1920s. Before this, in 1921, William Gray had bought it to be used as a convalescent home for his ship builders. Mr T W Pinkney then bought it and turned it into a country club. However, during the Second World War the army took it over and stationed troops there, including officers from the minesweepers. During the late 1940s it was converted by Vaux Breweries into the Staincliffe Hotel.

Farewell to Revd. Mortimer

Revd. Mortimer was keen to establish a parish hall, with three main uses: for the Young Men's Society, as a reading-room for the older parishioners, and as a parish hall for general purposes. He set out the scheme, but before he could finish it he left Holy Trinity. Fortunately his successor took up the challenge.

The very popular Revd. Mortimer left Seaton in 1894 to take up a post at St Cuthbert's Church, Darlington. However, the marriage registers for Seaton Carew show that he returned to Holy Trinity in 1896 to officiate at the wedding of William Scott Lithgo and Hannah Evans. The report in the Northern Daily Mail of his leaving presentations gave a flavour of his popularity, indicating that the parishioners regarded him as a model vicar. They must have been sorry to lose him after only 4 years' service. Revd. Mortimer was presented with a book containing the signatures of nearly 350 parishioners, a picture of the church and a silver tobacco box with an inscription on it.

The tobacco box gave away a secret that many did not know, that he was a smoker. Revd. Mortimer was amused by this. In his leaving speech he thanked the parishioners, showing gratitude for the personal friendships he had formed and the help he had received from the churchwardens during his time as vicar. He made special mention of the choir, saying that it was not always easy for forty people to work together without friction, but that any unpleasantness which had arisen had always proved to be merely temporary. He spoke of the choir's loyalty to himself and the church, and his belief that the choir was privileged to lead the praises of the congregation. Revd. Mortimer urged them all to "*try and be influenced always by the highest motives, and to set before themselves the highest ideal of worship*".

A separate presentation was made by the Young Men's Society, in which he had been very closely involved as its president. From a small membership in its early days, it now totalled nearly 80 members. In his speech, Revd. Mortimer referred to the proposed parish hall, noting that no provision had been made in it for the young women of the village to meet together. He promised to raise this with his successor, to try to arrange for a corner of the building to be devoted to the use of the girls, in order that they too might meet in a social way. So equality was alive and well in 1894, but if Revd. Mortimer's wishes were carried out, the girls only got a corner of the hall!

Revd. Mortimer was another example of a clergyman serving at Seaton who had an interest in education, for he became chairman of the Darlington School Board and Treasurer to the Diocesan Education Fund. He was described in the Northern Echo as "*a man of moderate views, earnest for the wellbeing of his parishioners and townsfolk; and with no great flourish but steady persistency he held aloft the torch of truth. He won much genuine esteem from all parties and sects.*"

He died in 1905 as a result of malignant lung problems, which he had tried to overcome the previous year by spending three months in New Zealand where his brother lived. After returning to England and realising he was not well enough to serve properly, he resigned the living at Darlington, but only a few weeks later he caught a chill and his condition worsened, leading to his death. He is buried in West Cemetery in Darlington.

CHAPTER 10 - TOWARDS THE TWENTIETH CENTURY

Reverend Charles Barnard Roderick Hunter Vicar 1894 – 1908

Revd Hunter

Charles Hunter was born in Canada at the Red River Settlement in Rupert's Land (now Winnipeg, Manitoba) on 9 September 1860. He was the youngest son of the Venerable James Hunter, a Church Missionary Society missionary and Archdeacon of Cumberland (in Canada), and Jean Ross Hunter. James' mission included translating biblical documents into the native American Indians' language, Cree.

Jean suffered ill health, and doctors recommended a move to England. In 1865, the family emigrated and James became vicar at Bayswater, London. James died first in 1882. Jean moved to the north of England with their clergyman son Charles and lived with him and his family for the rest of her life. The air in England obviously suited her, since she survived her husband, dying in Hartlepool in 1910 at the age of 87.

Educated at Trinity College, Cambridge, Charles obtained his B.A. in the same year that his father died. He received his theological education at the London College of Divinity, and was ordained deacon in 1884 and priest in 1885. He then moved to Yorkshire where he was curate at Brafferton until 1894. He then came to Seaton Carew and served until 1908. The parishioners of Brafferton gave him an illuminated manuscript bound in red leather to commemorate the occasion of his appointment to Seaton Carew.

In the same year that he arrived at Seaton, Charles married Elsie Campbell (née Dickson) of Edinburgh, who was 12 years his junior. They had a daughter Anne born in 1901.

Revd. Hunter organised the installation of a stone pulpit into the church, and offered the previous pulpit to the Mission Church. He presided over the Annual Meeting of the British & Foreign Bible Society when it was held at Seaton Carew in 1894 which included a talk illustrated by a Magic Lantern projector. The following poster is held by the Canadian Archives Service:

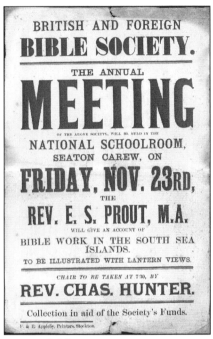

Bible society meeting

In 1895 Revd. Hunter changed the practice operated by John Lawson of not charging for any burials. While there were still no charges for local people, a resolution was passed that a fee of £10 be charged for burial in the churchyard of persons dying beyond the boundaries of the parish. There were exceptions: the fee would be waived if someone was born in the parish but died elsewhere, or if someone had already purchased a parcel of ground in the churchyard, or if it was a husband whose wife was already buried there or vice versa.

A permanent flagstaff was erected in the tower in 1897. At the PCC meeting, a proposal was put forward for increasing pew rents in order to raise funds for a Jubilee thanks offering for the Living of Seaton Carew. A special meeting of pew holders took place in April 1897 and a decision was taken unanimously to double the pew rents as a small addition to the value of the Living, benefiting Revd. Hunter directly.

In 1899 Revd. Hunter achieved the completion of the new building to house the Men's Club that Revd. Mortimer had established. It was built on a portion of the Vicarage Garden just to the north of the Parish Hall and connected to it by a doorway. The Vicar and Churchwardens were nominated as Trustees. On the East Front there was an inscribed stone which read:

"Seaton Carew Men's Club
This stone was laid by the Revd.
F.W. Mortimer M.A. on Wednesday August 2nd 1899
C.B.Hunter M.A. Vicar"

It was fitting that Revd. Mortimer was invited back to perform the laying of the foundation stone, since it was his idea to erect the building.

In 1900 some substantial repairs were done to the church, and a licence had to be obtained from the Bishop of Durham to hold services in the National School, as there was no other consecrated church in the parish. The churchwardens' annual accounts in 1903 included items such as the organist's salary (£40 per year), organ blower (£2 15s), gas and coke £24 2s 4d, and various charitable donations including the RNLI, Missions to Seamen, Waifs and Strays, National Schools, CMS and Sons of Clergy (daughters were not supported, presumably as they were expected to secure their future through marriage).

Double storey hall plans
Durham County Record Office
EP/SC4/33

Durham County Record Office holds some pen and ink architects' drawings for an extension to the parish hall and school for Revd. Hunter. These are interesting because the plans were for a two-storey building. Obviously this was never achieved, as it has only ever been a single storey building. Part of the set of drawings is reproduced here, by permission of Durham County Record Office.

Revd. Hunter's service to the lifeboats was recognised by the

Royal National Lifeboat Institute in 1905, when he was presented with a Binocular Glass *"bearing a suitable inscription as a slight recognition of your valuable and highly esteemed cooperation in the Lifeboat Cause whilst holding the office of Honorary Secretary of the Seaton Carew Branch during the last eleven years".*

In 1908 Revd. Hunter became vicar of St. Paul's, West Hartlepool, where he raised the funds to enable the new Church of St Luke to be erected. In addition to his clerical duties he volunteered as a member of the West Hartlepool School Board and Board of Guardians.

At the start of the Great War, Revd. Hunter was appointed as Chaplain to the Forces of West Hartlepool. In the following year he became Rector of Ryton, but had to resign in 1929 on account of ill health. He retired to Hexham, where he joined the local bowling club as a hobby. He died in 1930 and was honoured with a funeral service at Hexham Abbey.

CHAPTER 11 – THE SHADOW OF WAR

Revd. Charles Falkland Bickmore – vicar 1909 – 1917

Revd Bickmore

Charles Bickmore was born in 1862 at Kenilworth in Warwickshire, one of nine children born to parents Revd. William and Gertrude Bickmore. His first job was as a school tutor in Reigate. He married Ethel Stobart of Witton-le-Wear in 1882 at Cockermouth, Cumbria. A graduate of Cambridge University, he was ordained at Hereford in 1886. He held positions at Hereford and Husborne Crawley (Bedfordshire) and was Secretary of the Church Missionary Society for 9 years, before coming to Seaton Carew in 1909. He and Ethel had 5 children, but sadly their first son Hugh died when only 15 days old in 1892.

By the time Revd. Bickmore arrived, the first part of a new Esplanade had been opened at Seaton and more houses had been built. The Cooperative Society had opened branches of its grocery and butchery businesses. The Zinc Works was opened, with a railway for goods and fifty houses for the workers.

In researching his history of Seaton Carew, Derek Hornby discovered that during Revd. Bickmore's time, two Sunday Schools operated – one for children of the gentry, in the Vicarage, and one for other children in the church. Although the children attended the same school, they were sworn to secrecy about the separation of the Sunday Schools. Even the teachers were unaware, and the situation only came to light when one of them, Bertha Bulmer, discovered what was going on and resigned. In those days the gentry had a lot of influence on the vicar; Revd. Bickmore may not have felt he had much choice but to obey their wishes.

Revd. Bickmore was also behind the establishment of Holy Trinity Football Club, which still exists today, although there is no direct link to the church. He was assisted in this by "Holy Joe" Ibbotson, who later took holy orders.

In 1909 there was a change in the patronage arrangements for the church. Andrew Sherlock Lawson, great-grandson of Barbara Isabella Lawson the founder of Holy Trinity, agreed to transfer over the "advowson" (perpetual right of patronage) to the Bishop of Durham. This was a tactic designed to make it easier to award additional funding from the Ecclesiastical Commissioners, with a view to *making better provision for the cure of souls in the parish*.

A copy of the parish magazine from 1910 has survived:

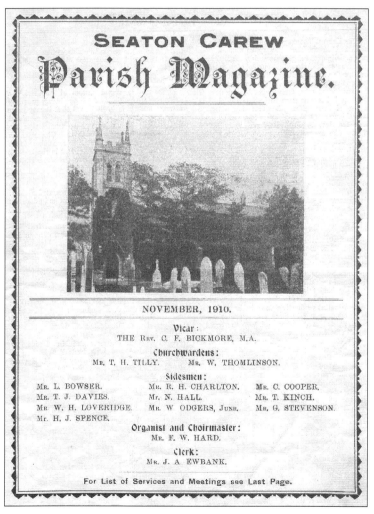

1910 magazine front

The back page of this magazine tells us that a rather complicated pattern of services was in place. While there was a regular 10.45 am morning service and a 6.30 pm evening service, communion services varied. This also reveals the number of associations that were still maintained by the church:

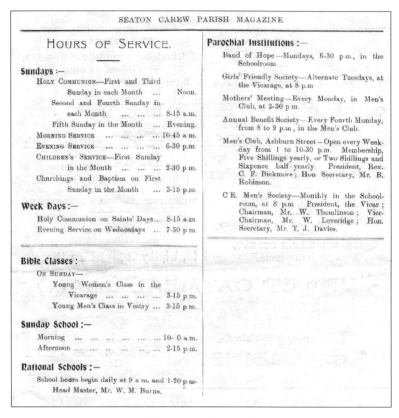

SEATON CAREW PARISH MAGAZINE.

HOURS OF SERVICE.

Sundays :—

HOLY COMMUNION—First and Third
    Sunday in each Month ... Noon.
    Second and Fourth Sunday in
      each Month ... ... 8-15 a.m.
    Fifth Sunday in the Month ... Evening.
MORNING SERVICE ... ...10-45 a.m.
EVENING SERVICE ... ... 6-30 p.m.
CHILDREN'S SERVICE—First Sunday
    in the Month ... ... 2-30 p.m.
Churchings and Baptism on First
    Sunday in the Month ... 3-15 p.m.

Week Days :—

Holy Communion on Saints' Days... 8-15 a.m.
Evening Service on Wednesdays ... 7-30 p.m.

Bible Classes :—

ON SUNDAY—
    Young Women's Class in the
      Vicarage ... ... 3-15 p.m.
    Young Men's Class in Vestry ... 3-15 p.m.

Sunday School :—

Morning ... ...10- 0 a.m.
Afternoon ... ... 2-15 p.m.

National Schools :—

School hours begin daily at 9 a.m. and 1-20 p.m.
Head Master, Mr. W. M. Burns.

Parochial Institutions :—

Band of Hope—Mondays, 6-30 p.m., in the
    Schoolroom.

Girls' Friendly Society—Alternate Tuesdays, at
    the Vicarage, at 8 p.m

Mothers' Meeting—Every Monday, in Men's
    Club, at 2-30 p.m.

Annual Benefit Society—Every Fourth Monday,
    from 8 to 9 p.m., in the Men's Club.

Men's Club, Ashburn Street – Open every Week-
    day from 1 to 10-30 p.m. Membership,
    Five Shillings yearly, or Two Shillings and
    Sixpence half-yearly. President, Rev.
    C. F. Bickmore ; Hon Secretary, Mr. B.
    Robinson.

C E. Men's Society—Monthly in the School-
    room, at 8 p.m President, the Vicar ;
    Chairman, Mr. W. Thomlinson ; Vice-
    Chairman, Mr. W. Loveridge ; Hon.
    Secretary, Mr. T. J. Davies.

1910 magazine back

Inside the magazine, we are told that the Church of England Men's Society had a meeting with a lantern lecture on "Changing China". However, the vicar bemoaned the low attendance, which resulted in a collection for the speaker of only ten shillings:

"What is it which makes the Seatonians so loath to attend any lecture or entertainment or meeting on a weeknight? It is very discouraging to those who organise these gatherings and most disheartening to the gentlemen and others who, at considerable trouble, attend to speak, etc. The next meeting of a similar kind will be held on Tuesday November 8th, at 7.30, in the Schoolroom, when the Vicar will give a Lantern Lecture on "Persia – A Land of Pain".

Original South Chancel windows

Salvator Mundi

St Peter

St Paul

John Lawson memorial window

To the glory of God and in memory of the Revd. John Lawson M.A. for
55 years Vicar of this Parish who died 10th August 1890.
This window is erected by Parishioners and friends.

Anna and Jane Wray memorial window

Anna Wray died ye 9th Dec A.D. 1843
Jane Wray died ye 12th May A.D. 1856

Anna Maria Fawcus memorial window

In memory of Anna Maria wife of Robert Fawcus Esq.
died May 5th 1871 aged 50

Ralph Thompson Walker memorial window

To the glory of God and in memory of Ralph Thompson Walker who
died 12th September 1876.
This window is erected by his widow.

Guthe memorial window

Erected by Barbara Mildred Guthe
In memory of her parents
Ann Guthe died April 3rd 1917
And Julius Ernst Guthe died June 27th 1917

Thomlinson memorial window

This sounds like a warning to parishioners that they had better get themselves to the next meeting, when their vicar would be the one that had taken the trouble to put together a talk for their benefit. Revd. Bickmore also had something to say about confetti at weddings:

"The rather stupid custom of smothering a bridal party with confetti is being generally abandoned. It is to be hoped that it may cease in Seaton. At all events it is earnestly requested that confetti be not thrown anywhere near the Church door. It gives the Church Cleaner much difficulty to clear up, and let it be remembered that Church Cleaners are not recognised in the table of fees, and she is not always remembered gratuitously."

The 1911 census shows 12 people living at the vicarage: Charles, his wife Ethel, children Amy, Gilbert, Margaret, and Charles, plus Revd. Bickmore's sister Amelia, a governess, cook, two housemaids and a 14 year old girl recorded as a boarder.

In 1912 there was a government inquiry into "The Sanitary Circumstances and Administration of the Borough of West Hartlepool". The report noted that *"Seaton Carew is a favourite suburban, almost rural, resort, but though fairly satisfactory in appearance along the main streets, it has unsatisfactory houses, courts and privy middens behind. The village is of ancient date, and there is much need of systematic sanitary inspection."*

However, there was no chance to put this right, as the country was plunged into war not long afterwards.

Around this time, it was becoming apparent that the church school, which had been built in 1844 and enlarged forty years later, was now too small given the size of the population. In 1913 Revd. Bickmore started a fund raising drive with a target of £6,500. The vicar gave a site from his glebe land for the new school and playground. A drain was laid in preparation for the project, running through the vicarage gardens past the church, in order to access the public sewer; even this had to be paid for by voluntary contributions of £85. This was essential, but it was not a particularly glamorous item to seek donations for.

However, like other plans, the work on the school had to be put to one side soon afterwards, when in 1914 Revd. Bickmore and the parishioners of Seaton Carew experienced the start of the Great War. The village was directly affected by the conflict. An airstrip was created on open land to the south of Seaton Carew at the southern end of Brenda Road near what is now

Stephenson Industrial Estate and Hunter House Farm. The airfield had a seaplane shed, two canvas hangers and associated buildings such as a wireless hut, flight commander's office, armoury, guard house and bomb stores. Over 100 personnel were located there. Seaplanes were kept in Seaton Channel and their station later became attached to the airfield.

One wartime incident must have been frightening for the townspeople. A group of four Zeppelin airships attacked the north east coast in on 27th November 1916. One of these, the L34 commanded by Korvettenkapitan Max Dietrich, crossed the coast at Blackhall Rocks at 12.30 am, dropping 16 bombs on West Hartlepool which killed 4 people and injured around 17 others. Indeed, the school log records that the village was in panic and the decision was taken not to open the school that day. This must have left a deep impression on the children, as on other occasions attendance suffered after an airship attack.

This Zeppelin was caught in a searchlight to the west of Hartlepool. It was spotted by Lieutenant Ian Vernon Pyott, the pilot of a biplane based at the Seaton Carew aerodrome, who chased it for five miles, and shot at it. The L34 Zeppelin, which was flying too low to escape, caught fire. Engulfed in flames, it fell into the sea at the mouth of the River Tees about a mile east of the Heugh lighthouse on Hartlepool Headland. All the crew perished, while the other Zeppelins made their escape.

The bodies of two of the Zeppelin airmen were washed up on 11th January 1917, and were buried in the churchyard at Holy Trinity. It was not possible to identify them after so long in the sea, so they were recorded on the gravestone as unknown German soldiers.

However, the German War Graves Commission's policy was that there should be a single burial place for Germans. They therefore arranged for the bodies to be disinterred and transferred to the Military Cemetery at Cannock Chase in July 1962. The inscription on each gravestone reads "Ein Unbekannter Deutscher Soldat" (an unknown German soldier).

Revd. Bickmore left in 1917 to become vicar of St Peter's Bishop Auckland. He died in 1947 at the age of 85 in Durham. His daughter Mrs Lillingstone gave a gift to Holy Trinity in his memory, consisting of a private communion set of a chalice, glass flagon, and paten in a case.

CHAPTER 12 – FAMILY MEMORIALS 1890 – 1917

Tobias Henry Tilly

This large brass Eagle Lectern was donated by Tobias Henry Tilly in 1891, when Revd. Mortimer was vicar of Holy Trinity. This is a beautiful piece of furniture, which holds the lectionary book and is used every week for readings.

The inscription reads:

Eagle lectern

> *"Ad Dei Gloriam DD*
> *Tobias Henricus Tilly*
> *1891"*

Tobias Henry Tilly was the founder of a well-known Hartlepool law firm and lived in Church Street, Seaton Carew. He was born in Melbourne, Australia in 1847 but moved to England as a young man and lived in Cornwall, which was where his ancestors had lived. In 1872 he married Onora Tilly from Cornwall, whose father also had the name of Tobias Henry Tilly, but who had died by the time of his daughter's marriage. Onora and Tobias were cousins, through their fathers Tobias Henry and William Parker Tilly being brothers, both sons of Captain John Tilly.

By 1881 the couple had moved to Church Street in Seaton Carew; they had seven children, but sadly two of them, Charles Wynn Tilly and John Tilly, died in the First World War. Both sons are commemorated in separate memorials.

Tobias, who was more commonly known as Henry or Harry, was a member of the Parochial Church Council. He formed a partnership with another lawyer, Edward Turnbull, and as Turnbull & Tilly Public Notaries, they dealt mainly with shipmasters' claims. The firm was amalgamated after his death with several other companies and now trades in Hartlepool as Tilly Bailey & Irvine (TBI). Law was the profession for many of the Tilly family.

Tobias Henry Tilly

Onora died in 1926 aged 78 and Tobias died in 1931 at the age of 84; both are buried at Holy Trinity. His son Tobias also became heavily involved in the life of the church at Seaton Carew, as a PCC member for many years and as a church warden between 1923 and 1928. He was also Manager of the church school. Sadly he died the year after his father, aged 57.

Mary Hudson

The current reredos (the wooden panel behind the altar) was installed in 1903, designed by Jones and Willis Ltd of London at a cost of £30. The inscription on the front reads:

"In memory of Mrs Mary Hudson
Who worshipped in this Church for upwards of 50 years."

Reredos, cross and candlesticks

Mary Hudson (née Sharp) was born in 1838; by the 1850s she was living in Seaton Carew with her husband Joseph Hudson, who was a coal and timber merchant. Joseph died in the 1850s and Mary became a lodging house keeper to support her young family. She eventually moved to Newcastle to live with her daughter Mary Blanche, who married Charles Saundersone. Mary died in September 1903 and is buried in Holy Trinity churchyard.

A faculty was required even to place two brass candlesticks and two plain brass vases upon the reredos; on the application for the reredos, the vicar had to own up to the fact that these had already been placed in church without having applied for a faculty. The two brass candlesticks are still there today (either side of the cross), noticeable by their twisted stems and claw-shaped tops.

Mary Woodward

Mary Woodward was born in Hull in 1846, one of seven children born to George Woodward and Hannah (née Mattewson). By 1851 her father, who was a grocer and merchant living in Hull, had died of Asiatic cholera, and her mother was running a lodging house in Seaton Carew. This must have been hard work with five children, of whom Mary was the second youngest.

Mary became a teacher, living with her mother at The Cliff. By 1891 she was living alone at The Cliff, recorded in the census as being the Mistress of the National School. She died in 1903 at the age of 57 while living at Bellerby Terrace, Hartlepool. Mary is remembered through an elaborate plaque on the north wall of the nave.

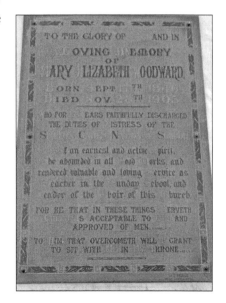

To the glory of God and in
loving memory of
Mary Elizabeth Woodward,
born Sept 17th 1846,
died Nov 28th 1903.
Who for 17 years faithfully discharged
the duties of Mistress of the Seaton
Carew National School.

John Cullen

A silver chalice was given to the church in memory of a soldier who lost his life in the Great War, inscribed:

"To the Glory of God
In loving memory of
John Cullen
2nd Lieut.
Argyle and Sutherland Highlanders
Killed in action
15th September 1916
Presented to Holy Trinity Church Seaton Carew."

John Cullen was born on 4 July 1895 to Robert Cullen, bank manager and Margaret Cullen, née Bryden. He was born in Brigand, Islay, Argyllshire. John had 4 brothers and 5 sisters, who were all minors at the time of his death. He went to school in Scotland at Islay and Edinburgh, and attended Glasgow University. He worked as an articled clerk before being commissioned into the army in August 1915.

John joined the 11th Battalion of the 13th Argyll & Sutherland Highlanders and was sent to France in June 1916. He only saw action for 3 months before being killed by friendly fire during the Battle of the Somme. It took a week for the telegram to arrive telling his family of his death. He was initially buried near Martinpuich Church near Arras in northern France, but was reburied at the Adanac Military Cemetery at Miraumont, which is a Commonwealth War Graves Commission burial ground.

John Cullen did not live in Seaton Carew, nor it appears did any of his family. However, Isabella Bird (niece of Rev John Lawson) and her sister Henrietta Bird were both friendly with a Miss Jane Cullen who lived in Edinburgh. Jane's father was George Downie Cullen and she had a brother who was a cotton broker. This is likely to be the connection that led to the chalice being given to Holy Trinity in memory of John Cullen.

CHAPTER 13 – FROM WAR TO PEACETIME

Revd. Frederick Batten Beaven – vicar 1917 – 1927

Frederick Beaven was born in 1872 at Tetbury in Gloucestershire, and married Isabella Collin in 1910 in Christchurch. He had previously been a curate at New Seaham and vicar at St John's Church Shildon. Revd. Beaven came to Holy Trinity in 1917, before the end of the Great War.

Revd Beaven

The experience of the war must have changed attitudes significantly and marked something of a turning point. The loss of many men of all ages from the community would have been very difficult, and the villagers would inevitably have looked to their vicar to support them through the time of change. Revd. Beaven was quick to pick up on the changes and is remembered as being more informal than previous vicars, wearing open necked shirts and encouraging the use of Christian names. He was immensely popular, especially with ordinary churchgoers. He installed a tennis court on the vicarage lawn and set up the Holy Trinity Tennis Club; the club lasted until the Second World War.

One of the new vicar's earliest decisions was to cease the practice of charging pew rents. He resolved that as soon as the value of the pew rents could be covered by other sources, they should be discontinued as the pews became vacant.

In December 1918, Revd. Beaven received a letter from the Vicar of St Oswald's Church, Revd. Robinson, offering the former Mission Church altar to Seaton church. A small brass plate recording this is on the north side of the altar, usually hidden below the altar frontal. By the time the altar was in use, sadly Rev. Robinson had passed away.

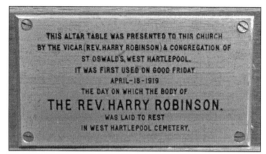

Altar plaque

There is also a painted declaration on the wooden panel at the north end of the altar, presumably relating to the original donation of the Mission Church altar:

"This altar is erected to the glory of God and in memory of Ellen Lydia Stuart who died March 12th 1890."

At the same time, a new East window was installed, with a generous donation from Barbara Mildred Guthe in memory of her parents Ann and Julius Ernst Guthe:

"To the Glory of God this East Window is erected

by Barbara Mildred Guthe

in loving memory of her parents

Ann Guthe who died April 3rd 1917

and Julius Ernst Guthe who died June 27th 1917"

More information on the Guthe family can be found in a later section on family memorials from this time.

The Parochial Church Council (PCC) had to ask the Diocese for permission (a "faculty") to remove the old window, and to build up about 3 feet of the lower part of this window in order to install the new window and altar table. Examination of the outside of the East wall today reveals a different coloured sandstone used to fill in the space; this is quite obvious when you look at it, but until I researched the church's history I had never noticed this detail.

Mrs Beaven played an important part in the life of the church. She became the first Girl Guide captain in the town, supported by Rosa and Lily Bulmer. A Guide hut was erected in 1918 in the north west corner of the vicarage garden near the Men's Club. This lasted until 1961 when the PCC decided it should be removed from the church grounds, because it was not in use and was in bad condition.

Revd. Beaven received an acknowledgement from the RNLI in 1919 for his contribution, together with the local lifeboat committee, in carrying out the work of the lifeboat station and fund raising for the big task of reconstruction after the war.

In February 1921 the Bishop of Durham, Dr Hensley Henson, visited Seaton Carew to dedicate the clock and bells (given by Col. Thomlinson), the brass tablet war memorial in church and a war memorial on The Green in the form of a Victoria Cross upon a shaft.

The tablet in the church bears the following inscription:

Pro Patria 1914 – 1919 To the Glory of God and in Grateful Memory of The Men and Women from the Village Who Served in the Great War. These Gave their Lives. Pro Deo. Pro Justitia. Pro Libertate.

Victor Ed E Bentley	Harry Waite	J A Norman Hessler
Clarence Birkenshaw	Harry Cass	Jack K M Hessler
George H Birkenshaw	Charles Davies	Percy Murray
Ralph Percival Booth	Arthur Foster	Wm McLaren
Francis Cecil Booth	Thos. Percival Guthe	James Frank Peet
Bert Carnall	Cecil Rudolph Guthe	Samuel Smith
Louis Charlton	Ernest M Harrison	Charles W Tilly
James Crilly	Luke Patchcott	John Tilly

The service began in church with the dedication of the bells and brass tablet, and a collection was taken in aid of the Cameron Hospital.

Left to right: Bishop's chaplain, Rev Beaven, Bishop of Durham, J Stevenson, AJ (Joe) Ibbotson, G Stevenson, a young Ken Morgan, Mrs Morgan, and W Bainbridge.

The congregation then proceeded to the stone cross memorial on The Green, as the previous photograph shows (going past the Waverley Café).

Once at The Green, the congregation sang "O God, our help in ages past" before the next part of the service began with the following prayer:

"Accept, we beseech Thee, O Lord God, this Memorial at our hands and bless it to the purpose for which it is erected. Grant that those who pass by it may be stirred by thankful remembrances of Thy Fatherly care and of the lives given on their behalf, that they may be moved to strive manfully for the advancement of Thy Kingdom of Light and Peace, of Righteousness and Love; through Jesus Christ our Lord. Amen."

The monument was unveiled by Colonel L Robson, who had shown bravery during the bombardment of Hartlepool and was awarded medals for his services.

The names of those from Seaton Carew who lost their lives in the war are also to be found on the Hartlepool War Memorial in the town centre.

Inter-parish tensions

One of the more entertaining sagas in Revd. Beaven's time was the matter of services held at the nearby community of Graythorp. Sir William Gray created an estate at Graythorp to house the shipbuilding workers he employed, but it did not have a church; it came under the parish of Greatham. It did however have a club, and early in 1921, the Committee asked Revd. Beaven if it might be possible to hold a service for all denominations at 6.30 pm on a Sunday there. Canon Macdonald the Rural Dean approved the proposal and it was set up.

Mr Hare, who was the agent for Wm Gray, wrote to Revd. Beaven to pass on the request. He also mentioned that a request had been made for *"a bit of Sunday School"* for the small number of children there. Mr Hare's view was that the basis for this request was *"anything O Lord for a bit of peace on Sunday afternoons"*, rather than a sense of piety or any desire for the children to receive religious instruction. The plea was successful, as later a Sunday school was opened at Graythorp.

However, the multi-denominational services did not quite suit the people of Graythorp, at least not in respect of the sermons delivered by Mr Hall, the lay reader who was sent to conduct the service. Correspondence between Mr Hare and Canon Macdonald indicates that Mr Hall had committed the crime of speaking for far too long:

"Dear Canon, Herewith letter I sent to Hall – I am sorry to have to send it but he's put everyone's backs up down there and done his best to spoil the whole thing. I hear he actually had to be stopped talking after ¾ of an hour!!

Yours, LS Hare.

Copy of letter enclosed:

Dear Mr Hall,

I regret to hear that your service was disturbed last Sunday evening but I am not surprised to hear so if what I hear is correct "that the service was not concluded until five minutes to eight".

I arranged with Canon Macdonald that this service should be to suit all denominations with plenty of hymns and a short address. The service in all not to take more than three quarters of an hour. The Club is supposed to be open at 6.30 but the members have allowed at my request an hour for this service and for the Club to be cleared and it is not open until 7.30 pm on Sundays. I was under the impression that you were aware of all this and cannot understand how you could allow last Sunday's service to go on for so long after the limit. If the three-quarter of an hour service does not suit Lay readers we better cancel them and only have a monthly service with an Ordained Minister. If you organise the Lay readers services will you please assure me that they will be over in three-quarters of an hour in future and that the address will not be more than ten to 12 minutes.

I am afraid last Sunday's incident has caused a good deal of disturbance though I am sorry to say so.

Yours faithfully

LS Hare

There is no record of what sort of disturbance Mr Hall had been faced with. Although the services did continue, presumably with a lay reader who was willing to keep his sermons short, this incident soured relationships between Graythorp Club and Seaton Church. When Revd. Beaven made an approach to use the club's recreation room, he was given short shrift and advised to lay low for a while.

As Graythorp grew, with around 250 adults and 150 children living there, Rev Beaven decided it would be better if there was an alternative form of accommodation for service. He wanted something which the clergy could control, rather than rely on Graythorp Club's goodwill, which had proved rather fragile. He identified one of a number of 60 by 20 feet huts lying unoccupied at the bottom of the village, which could be transferred to a suitable site at the top. An agreement was negotiated so that Wm Gray's company would do the work to move the hut and set it up, and Seaton Church would reimburse them for the costs of £30 and then pay a nominal rent of £1 per year plus a quarterly charge for lighting.

The vicar of Greatham at this time, John H Batten, had little interest in Graythorp, despite it being within his parish, unlike Revd. Beaven, who proposed a Welfare Scheme at Graythorp. To be fair to Greatham, having a community allocated to your parish when there was no accessible road to it was not exactly ideal. Revd. John Batten relayed the disgruntled attitude from Greatham in a letter, saying

> *"To work Graythorp from Greatham is absolutely impossible. It will be a good thing when it is cut off and made into a separate Parish, as I suppose it will be one day.*
>
> *It is very difficult to get the people here to take any interest at all in Graythorp. Financially they can do nothing as they are doing all they can to make up the income here to a living wage.*
>
> *As you know this living is only £230 a year.*
>
> *I feel very strongly that the Grays ought to do something to help as they are giving the Vicar here extra work and responsibility."*

Revd. Batten did however provide a small grant of £10 to the Lay Readers Association, funded by the Greatham Hospital Trustees, in recognition of the work its members had done at Graythorp. Others must have improved upon the performance of Mr Hall.

In April 1923 the Trustees of Greatham Hospital voted the sum of £35 to be handed to the Vicar of Greatham for clerical assistance for work in the parish. The cheque was sent to Rev Beaven as he was now responsible for the working of Graythorp. It was decided it would be used for a Lay Reader at Graythorp. As we will see later, this proposal also ran into problems, which were not discovered until several years afterwards.

Grave business

It proved difficult at times to get burial space in Holy Trinity's graveyard. A Miss Frances Elizabeth Richards from Harrogate died in December 1922 and was buried at Seaton. The correspondence from a firm of solicitors to Revd. Beaven indicates this must have been done without the vicar knowing:

> *"It was absolutely essential for the late Miss Richards' funeral to take place quickly, had it been possible more notice would have been given. This was, under the circumstances, impossible. The Executors tender to you their apologies for any inconvenience which may have been caused.*
>
> *We appreciate how important it is to preserve burying space for the Seatonians, and the same as having regard to the close proximity of Seaton Carew to West Hartlepool.*

In a somewhat similar case in which the writer was concerned, the position was met, by making a charge for the burial of non-parishioners, the monies so received being funded and satisfied for the purchase of additional burying ground. This worked with great success, and this particular case, all the parties in question are practically Seatonians.

Mr Richards the husband, who was so many years Vicar of Hunwick, in the County of Durham, lived and died at Seaton Carew, and his wife the late Mrs Richards and all the members of the family, lived for many years at Seaton Carew, in which place they always took a deep interest, which has been tangibly shown on more than one occasion, and particularly by the late Miss Richards, who left a legacy of £500 to the National Lifeboat Institution, which sum would have been left to the particular branch of the Institution at Seaton Carew, had not that branch been abolished before her death.

Beyond this, it will be within your recollection, that a considerable sum we believe (and here we speak from memory) £10 was paid over, on the enclosure of the ground.

However, care will be taken in the maintenance of the graves and the monuments, that there is no interference with any adjacent graves, everything will be treated with the greatest respect, and with the greatest care."

The letter also confirms that space has been left in the grave for the interment of Miss Cook, an old servant of the family, who was a beneficiary of Miss Richards' will. The case made by the solicitors was not only that her long residence with the family virtually made her a Seatonian, but for added measure she was a direct descendant of Captain James Cook. The plea obviously worked, as Frances Abia Cook was indeed buried in Holy Trinity after her death in 1924 at the age of 85.

The Bulmer family

The Bulmer family are one of the oldest Seaton families, with baptisms recorded in the then mother parish of Stranton as early as the 1600s. Professions undertaken by family members over the years were Tees pilot, mariner, shoemaker, cotton mill worker, and boarding house keeper. They were loyal to the lifeboat cause, with several Bulmers serving throughout its history.

Rosa Bulmer was a notable supporter of Holy Trinity during Revd. Beaven's time and beyond. As well as helping Mrs Beaven with the Girl Guides, Rosa gave many years of service to the Parochial Church Council. She was a teacher at Seaton School and later at Lynnfield. She was the first lady who was asked to be the secretary of the PCC and held this post for many years, as well as being a school governor at Seaton School. Rosa organised the Free Will Offerings and the flower rota, and was Electoral Roll secretary up to her death in June 1984.

Rosa Bulmer with a young
Bob Bulmer

Rosa was born Sarah Rosamund Bulmer, to Robert Bulmer and Jane (née Dunning). Although both her parents were born in Seaton Carew, Rosa and her siblings Lily and James were born in Bolton, Lancashire, where her father was working in a cotton mill. They later returned to Seaton Carew and Robert became a school caretaker. He died in 1943.

Rosa's grandfather was Joseph Bulmer, 1842-1882, one of 10 children born to Robert and Elizabeth Bulmer, who were thus responsible for setting up quite a dynasty. Robert was born in Seaton Carew in 1816; his wife came from Hexham. Joseph nearly came to grief in a boating accident in 1865 with John Lithgo, and had to be rescued by Jim Franklin and William Sewell who rowed out in a canoe at great personal risk; the rescuers were recognised by the RNLI. We do not know whether this was behind

Rosa's mother Jane Ellen Bulmer (75th birthday) with grandchildren Jane Harrison, Bob Bulmer, Judith Bulmer, Elizabeth Harrison, and Gwynneth Bulmer

Joseph's later action in joining the lifeboat crew, but he was one of several Bulmers to serve in this capacity.

New school building

Revd. Beaven had come to Seaton from St John's Church in Shildon, where he was involved in the Metcalfe Charity which raised funds for the school. He was another clergyman who was committed to education, and set about making a reality of the plans set in motion by his predecessor Revd. Bickmore to build a new school for Seaton Carew. The site chosen, next door to the church, was where the schoolmaster's cottage was, and this was to be demolished in order to make way for the school.

Once the war was over, a committee was formed, chaired by Tobias Harry Tilly, to resurrect the fund raising efforts for the new school building. This took a considerable time; by 1925 there was a shortfall of £2,000, so a Bazaar Committee was formed to raise the balance. There was considerable pressure on its members to succeed: the two foundation stones for the school had already been laid on July 24th 1924 by Colonel Thomlinson and Tobias Harry Tilly. These can still be seen on the south side of Holy Trinity Primary School, although the lettering is quite worn.

The school provided education for 260 children and the new building was opened by the Lord Bishop of Jarrow on 25th May 1925. The final cost was approximately £6,000.

Revd. Beaven left Seaton in 1927 to become vicar of Ruckringe in Canterbury. His wife Isabella died in August 1944 and he died four months later in December 1944. He was remembered by Canon James Booth in the following tribute:

"Mr Beaven was a man greatly beloved by the people of Seaton Carew, and Mrs Beaven also shared the affection of our people. Together they did a great work in our Parish and have left a warm place in the hearts of all who knew them. Our Church School is an abiding memorial to their Ministry, and their love of the parish is manifest in their desire that their mortal remains should be laid together in our Church Yard... May God give us grace to follow their good examples to serve faithfully that when our work is done we may attain to the Rest which remained for the people of God" (source: Derek Hornby).

It is notable that despite having been born in Gloucestershire and ending his clerical career in Canterbury, Revd. Beaven was buried at Holy Trinity Seaton Carew. He and his wife are both buried in the same grave as Isabella's mother Elizabeth Collin.

Revd. Beaven bequeathed the sum of £10 to the vicar and churchwardens of Seaton Carew "*as a thank offering for the happy years spent there and in order that they might purchase something for the use of the church there*". The church inventory records that a Bible was purchased.

CHAPTER 14 – FAMILY MEMORIALS 1918 – 1927

Guthe family

The most significant feature of Holy Trinity, its beautiful East window, was given by the Guthe family. This triple window is a representation of the baptism of Jesus Christ, his crucifixion and the ascension to heaven. This is shown on page 91.

The windows are the work of Jones and Willis, a major ecclesiastical outfitters and decorating firm. Their name is inscribed in the bottom corner of the right hand window. Jones and Willis had outlets in London, Birmingham and Liverpool, and specialised in metalwork, printing, church robes, linen and embroideries. After 1880 they began making stained glass and continued in business almost up to the Second World War. Although thoroughly traditional in style, their window glass was always reasonably well drawn and crafted, but generally regarded as unexciting.

The inscriptions on the glass are:

Baptism: This is My Beloved Son

Crucifixion: It is Finished

Ascension: I Ascend unto My Father

The baptism window also has the inscription "Ecce Agnus Dei" – Behold the Lamb of God. Jesus is shown symbolically in only a few inches of water rather than the total immersion that would have been the case. The crucifixion window shows the banner INRI on the cross. The I is a representation of a J and the abbreviation stands for "Jesus of Nazareth King of the Jews".

The Guthe family were a well-respected shipbuilding family. Julius Ernst Guthe was born in 1856 in Leipzig, Saxony in Germany. He came to West Hartlepool in 1875, securing a job at Messrs Cory Lohden & Co., and three years later he married Ann Sharper. The 1881 census records him as being a foreign correspondent, a naturalised British subject, living at Bird's Field (near Green Terrace) in Seaton Carew, with his wife Ann, one son Friedrich aged 1, and a servant.

Julius' wife Ann was born in 1860 in Hartlepool to Dixon Taylor Sharper and Barbara Ridley Sharper née Allen. The Guthes had 7 children: four sons – Friedrich (born 1880), Thomas (1883), Julius Ernst (1885), Cecil (1889) and three daughters – Barbara (1881), Annie (1886) and Audrey (1907). Barbara, who gave the window to Holy Trinity, died unmarried at the age of 54 in Darlington.

Julius Ernst seems to have had varying fortunes. In 1889 he joined a Mr Murdoch to form a company, Guthe Murdoch & Co, ship owners, agents and coal exporters, but it was wound up after only a year and Mr Guthe left the country. He was reported in the Leeds Mercury as having disappeared owing £18,880. While he only had £670 in assets, he was expecting to make a lot of money from a valuable coal contract. The newspaper informed its readers that Julius' financial situation was due to gambling in pig iron warrants. This was a system of trading which held some risk as prices could change, but it was not illegal, as regulations on stocks and shares dealings did not cover it.

However, by 1899 Julius' fortunes had certainly improved significantly. He returned to England in 1892 and created a new company J E Guthe & Co., gradually acquiring a fleet of ships. Ralph Ward Jackson had founded the West Hartlepool Steam Navigation Company in 1856, the year of Julius' birth. This company amalgamated with Messrs. J E Guthe & Co., with a share issue. Julius became the managing director and Sir Christopher Furness was chairman.

The amalgamated company took control of a fleet of 17 steamers, plus contracts for completing another four. The steamers ran between West Hartlepool, Hamburg and Gothenburg.

The fleet was valued at £341,500, which at current prices would be over £34.5m, and the accountants confidently predicted good profits for the company. One can only wonder at the determination and hard work that must have made such a turnaround possible. Tobias Harry Tilly, another well-known Seaton Carew gentleman associated with Holy Trinity as we have seen, was a Trustee of the Company.

In 1904 Furness sold his shareholding to Julius, who then became Chair. By this time the family was living at Dinsdale Lodge, a large house in Station Lane. Julius was a respected member of the golf club, and represented the Seaton Ward on the West Hartlepool Council, although he resigned from the latter position when he became chairman of his company. He became chairman of several important local marine insurance companies and other associations, and was also a JP in County Durham. He was described as a man of splendid business capacity with keen commercial instincts.

Julius was a member of the Hartlepools Port & Harbour Commissioners, and at the outbreak of the First World War, being very conscious of his German nationality, he tried to resign from the Board. His resignation was rejected – a sign of the respect his fellow board members felt towards him.

During the First World War airmen lodged at Dinsdale House, and other properties in Seaton were requisitioned to house army personnel: the swimming baths, the Staincliffe (for a camp and training ground), The Marine Hotel (for stores), the Golf House and several other houses including Ashprington in Station Lane (used as the Battalion HQ), and 1 Sea View Terrace. Horses were accommodated at the Seaton Hotel. The golf course was closed; trenches were built along the sand dunes and German POWs were put to task building the road to Port Clarence.

The Guthe family bought a large estate as their family home: Kepwick Hall, Kepwick near Thirsk. The family still owns the Memorial Chapel at Kepwick. There is an interesting link to Peter Stephenson, the chairman of the company Able UK which was responsible for bringing the "ghost ships" to Hartlepool for dismantling. Mr Stephenson has also lived at Kepwick Hall – in 2002 he was shot at by armed intruders in his garden there.

Sadly one of Julius Guthe's sons, Thomas Percival Guthe, was killed in 1916 at the age of 32 in Le Touquet in France in the war, after being wounded in action. He was buried in France. A year later Julius' wife Ann also died. Julius himself was in failing health, and his family felt that his distress at this double blow hastened his death. He died in 1917 at the age of 60, only six months after his wife, and left a large sum in his will: more than £577,000.

Julius' obituary noted that he "*was the essence of geniality and he will be greatly missed by a very wide circle of friends who held him in the highest esteem. The many charitable organisations in the district lose by his death a warm sympathiser and supporter. Since the war broke out the soldiers at Hartlepool, West Hartlepool and Seaton Carew also found in him a very generous friend, whilst the many war charities have been cordially supported by him, though for the most part anonymously. Many people in Hartlepool & District owe much to him for a quiet helping hand in a time of stress.*"

A second Guthe son died in 1919 – Cecil Rudolph, who caught pnemonia while serving in the forces and died at Kepwick Hall. He was buried in Holy Trinity churchyard. Although he did not die in action, he is commemorated on the war memorial tablet in church.

Julius junior followed his father into the business, becoming a director of the companies, so was able to ensure continuity after his father's death. He too supported the local community, and featured in the Northern Daily Mail in March 1942 when he opened Hartlepool Warship Week and pledged a donation of £75,000 to the fund for adopting the destroyer HMS Ludlow. This was a repetition of his generous gesture for War Weapons Week and caused him to be referred to as the town's "fairy godfather". No one has recorded what he thought of this title.

Tilly family

Tobias Harry Tilly, who donated the eagle lectern, sadly lost two sons in the space of two months during the final year of the Great War. They are both named on the war memorial in church as well as the memorial on The Green in Seaton and on the Cenotaph in Victory Square Hartlepool.

Tilly plaque

Charles Wynn Tilly was born in Hartlepool in 1876 to Tobias Harry and Onora Tilly. He was a boarder at Repton School (an independent school) in Derbyshire, where he enjoyed country pursuits such as hunting, fishing, walking and climbing. The list of students also includes his elder brother Tobias H Tilly.

Charles decided not to follow his brothers into the legal profession, and after collecting an MA from Pembroke College Cambridge, he became a land agent for Sir William Gray at the Membland Estate near Noss Mayo, Plymouth. This was developed by Edward Baring, of Barings bankers, along with a church, post office and school. Sir William Gray, of the shipbuilding family from Hartlepool, bought the estate from the Barings in 1890, although he sold many of the buildings in 1915.

Charles Wynn Tilly

Charles is recorded in the 1901 census, aged 24, living near Totnes in Devon, with his sister May and a domestic servant. William Gray then asked Charles to transfer to the Thorp Perrow Estate near Bedale which he also owned. Charles moved to Snape, living in the castle there, and in 1908 he married Ruth Warmington in London. A daughter Joan was born in 1909. He became active in the church at Snape, chairing the PCC until the start of the Great War.

Charles applied for a commission with the Durham Light Infantry in October 1914 and was made a temporary Major in the County Battalion. He died in action in Northern France in 1918 at Ypres when the battalion were on their way back to their billet to wait for relief troops and a stray shell exploded among them. He was 41 years old. Charles is commemorated on the Ploegsteert Memorial in Belgium near the border with France.

He and his brother John are also remembered on the war memorials at the Cenotaph Hartlepool, The Green Seaton Carew and the memorial in Seaton church. Sir William Gray gave an institute building, which was

Tilly Institute, Noss Mayo

previously Charles' cottage, to the parish of Revelstoke at Noss Mayo in memory of Charles.

John Tilly was born in 1887 in Seaton Carew. Like Charles, he attended Repton School and in 1905 he entered Pembroke College Cambridge to study law; he was admitted to the bar in October 1911. He became a managing clerk in the family firm Turnbull and Tilly Solicitors in West Hartlepool.

When the war began, John was commissioned into the 8th Batallion Yorkshire Regiment in 1914, becoming a Lieutenant in 1915 and then Captain in 1916. Fighting in Northern France, he was wounded twice but recovered. In early 1917 Captain Tilly was involved at Ypres in the Battle of Messines and the Passchendaele offensive. The battalion was moved to the Italian Front at Rivalta in November 1917, and some months later they transferred to the Asiago Plateau, to the north of Venice.

On June 8th 1918 Captain John Tilly led a raid on the enemy line in the village of Morar but was severely wounded and died later that day. A fellow officer wrote, "The loss of Captain Tilly was greatly felt". He is buried in Barenthal Military Cemetery three miles south of Asiago.

When Revd. Beaven applied for the faculty to place the Tilly memorial tablet on the wall, he wrote to the Diocese to explain a rather sensitive situation that had developed:

Dear Mr Lazenby,

T H Tilly the solicitor, a man greatly respected, who has done a very great deal for the church here for many years, is now an old man but still very keen. He is a man of strong opinions, but withal of a kindly disposition beneath what has at first the appearance of a brusque appearance.

He lost two fine sons in the last year of the war. He feels the loss very much. He proposes putting up a mural tablet to them on the wall of the church. He has taken a long time to think it over with Mrs T and has now announced his decision.

The widow of one of the sons also wants to place another tablet to the memory of her husband so that he is in both. I don't like the idea at all, but between ourselves I daren't say so, nor do I want it opposed. The people here will no doubt pass the resolution for the faculty but I wondered if the Chancellor would have any hesitation in approving. If so I would like to break the news as early as possible to THT.

Will you be good enough to let me know if there is likely to be any objection. They have in mind, I understand, placing them one above the other on the wall near the seat which he used.

Sorry to bother you

Yours very sincerely F B Beaven

The approval from the Diocese said an application for a second tablet to one of the same individuals could not be entertained. However, there is a second tablet on the wall today, so permission must have eventually been given for this:

"In Loving Memory of Lt. Col Charles Wynn Tilly
Erected by his Widow, Ruth Tilly,
and their daughter Joan."

Colonel Sir William Thomlinson, D.L., J.P

Lt-Col. Sir William Thomlinson – two eras
Oil paintings held by Museum of Hartlepool

William Thomlinson was born in 1854 in Houghton-le-Spring, County Durham. He lived in Stockton for a time, where he impressed the community with his knowledge of foreign languages (learning Spanish within three months), and his literary abilities, which he demonstrated on subjects such as foreign politics and trade for the Daily Gazette and the Herald.

When quite young, he emigrated to the USA, and worked as a manager in the iron industry in Tennessee. A settlement was being formed there with a church, a school, and a newspaper. Having gained valuable experience in the industry, William returned to the north east in 1882 and took up the post of manager at the Seaton Carew Iron Company. The ironworks had not been in operation for some years, and he reconstructed and restarted them.

In 1882 he married Hannah Kirk (known as Nancy), the daughter of Thomas Kirk who owned the ironworks' controlling company the Carlton Iron Company. William joined the Carlton board and became Managing Director when his father-in-law died. Dorman Long & Co bought the Carlton Iron Company in 1920, making him a very wealthy man. Some locals of the time felt he was the nearest thing to a village squire; certainly he was regarded as a community leader.

An interview with the then Captain Thomlinson by the North Eastern Daily Gazette in 1894 gives some insight into how he ran the ironworks. He was being asked how his introduction of the eight hour day had gone. The reporter noted that this "frank and courteous gentlemen" had introduced the system to achieve a continuous process for charging the blast furnace to get uniform results for the smelting, and that initial signs were promising but had not quite come up to his expectations yet. His feeling was that if the men used their leisure time in studying betting news and wasting their money, it would be a disastrous change, but he hoped they would show common sense by using their extra time off to indulge in proper recreation such as gardening or other healthy recreation pursuits. One senses that the Captain was an optimist.

Captain Thomlinson further observed that as a rule the majority of men working in the blast furnace made good money and were not overworked under the new system, but they had to recognise he was in charge, and that they had to have good attendance. His expectations show an almost military approach – he needed an "attentive and steady set of men" who should work through the next shift if someone else didn't turn up through accident or sickness. If men were idle they would be dealt with by fines or a more summary type of discipline for frequent offenders.

The Captain took the opportunity presented by the press interview to push the cause of temperance, emphasising the difficulties caused by men with a failing for strong drink, and making it clear that they needed to be taught that no latitude would be allowed; men would be expected to be sober and controlled, and if they failed to carry out their duties, they must suffer. One gets the distinct impression the Colonel did not suffer fools gladly, which was probably one of the reasons for his success.

William and Nancy had a son Francis and four daughters: Daisy, Gladys, Kathleen and Aileen. They resided in Seaton Hall on The Green, which is now a nursing home. Original features such as the fireplaces and oak panelling can still be seen inside the building. Mr Thomlinson also owned Home Farm in Seaton, but did not work the land, instead employing a manager. An interest in local history led to him giving lectures on the subject, but unfortunately for us he did not make available any printed material.

Seaton Hall – home of the Thomlinson family

William became a significant political figure when he was elected to represent Seaton Carew on the West Hartlepool council as a Conservative. In 1897 he became a Justice of the Peace, frequently presiding over the magistrates' bench. Later he took up the Presidency of the Hartlepools Conservative Association. In 1909 he was appointed as a trustee of the Temperance Hall adjacent to the parish hall, having also established the Thomlinson Institute at Stranton to promote the cause of temperance.

Mr Thomlinson was heavily involved in the military, becoming an officer in the Durham Light Infantry. Although he volunteered for foreign service, this was not accepted and instead he was given responsibility for raising and training two battalions during 1914-16. He commanded several voluntary units engaged in the Coast Defence group for Durham during the last two years of the Great War, eventually rising to the rank of Lieutenant Colonel. His commitment was recognised with an appointment as Deputy Lieutenant of County Durham. He had a huge range of interests outside of work, with only a few examples being the YMCA, the Imperial Lads' Brigade, and the local volunteer movement.

In 1920 Colonel Thomlinson gave a generous gift to Holy Trinity of the chiming clock and the four bells in the tower, as a thanksgiving for his mercies and in memory of the fallen of the Great War of 1914-18.

Clock exterior

As you enter Holy Trinity, if you look up, you will see a commemorative plaque on the wall to the right of the staircase to the tower:

To the Glory of God
The Chiming Clock and Bells in this Tower
were erected in the year of our Lord 1920
by Lt Col W and Mrs Thomlinson of this parish
As a thanksgiving for His mercies and for the great deliverance
1914-1919
Te Deum Laudamus.

The clock was ordered by Mr H Lamb the Hartlepool clockmaker and purchased from William Potts & Sons Ltd of Leeds. It is a Cambridge quarter chiming clock fitted with a gravity escapement identical to the one used in the Palace of Westminster (known as Big Ben). A gravity escapement is a device that gives an impulse to the pendulum to keep the clock going.

Having been in touch with Michael Potts, of the Potts family, I wanted to see the mechanism, and climbed up the steps to the tower, accompanied by Father Paul our vicar. There is not much room up here, and you have to step carefully around the hatch, avoiding the ladder that goes right up to the bells themselves. There are two doors, the upper glazed sections of which open out in the fashion of a stable door, to reveal the clock's mechanism. There is a long pendulum with a heavy weight at one end.

Although the clock is not currently working, Father Paul demonstrated that it can operate, by lifting one of the levers. The cogs started to turn and a perfect chime filled the air – a magic moment.

There is another plaque on the mounting of the mechanism itself, which refers to the initials of Colonel Thomlinson and his wife together with a Latin inscription Te Deum Laudamus: "We praise you o God".

Interestingly, William Potts was an apprentice of Samuel Thompson of Darlington, the maker of the previous clock installed in 1841. Potts set up

Clock mechanism in the tower

his own business in 1833 at Pudsey near Leeds. The company became one of the most important makers of turret (exterior) clocks in Britain and exported timepieces abroad.

The new clock was set going on 31st December 1920. The dedication of the church clock and bells given by Colonel Thomlinson was carried out by the Bishop of Durham in February 1921 along with the dedication of the brass tablet in church commemorating the men of the parish who gave their lives in the war, and the war memorial on The Green, already mentioned.

Colonel Thomlinson also gave the pulpit and the font.

Pulpit

Font

Colonel Thomlinson retired from business in 1924 and travelled extensively, including trips to India, Africa and the Far East, where he developed an interest in collecting oriental 18th century porcelain and statues of Buddha and Hindu deities. He donated some of these to the Gray Art Gallery and Museum and his family donated the rest after his death. It was said that his home was more like a museum because of the quantity of artefacts displayed there.

During the period between the First and Second World Wars, Colonel Thomlinson became a considerable benefactor to the village. In 1922 he provided money and freehold land that he owned, to set up a Foundation Trust which built the Vesper Homes in Queen Street in 1924. These consisted of five houses, intended for his servants to retire to, including his maid Ada Roberts.

The inscription on the building reads:

To the Glory of God
as an enduring memorial of thanksgiving
this House of Rest was founded by
Lt. Col William Thomlinson JP DL
of this village.
Non Nobis Domine.

The Vesper Homes, Queen Street

Sadly Hannah Thomlinson died in 1926 while away from home in Middlesex, but she was brought back to Holy Trinity for burial.

Col. Thomlinson played a prominent part in the formation of the West Hartlepool Branch of the British Legion, reflecting his interest in the welfare of ex-Servicemen, and was a regular at the Legion parades. In 1936 he became president of the branch; in the same year he was knighted for his public services.

He was always a generous supporter of the church school at Seaton and also St Aidan's C of E school, and made a donation for the building of the swimming baths at Seaton. As well as his gifts to the museum, he made donations to the public library to enable them to purchase technical and scientific books. He served on various diocesan boards.

Col. Thomlinson's daughter Gladys married Charles L Wainwright, a manager at the Zinc Works. This brought two powerful industrial families together, creating something of a dynasty at the family home "Miamba" in Station Lane. Gladys became a JP like her father and she received an MBE for her work in local affairs. Charles also played an important part in the life of the church, assisting several clergy in decision making and playing a leading role in the PCC.

Francis Thomlinson, the Colonel's son, was a very keen photographer. He was also a supporter of Holy Trinity. In 1963 he left £500 to the vicar and wardens to use as needed for the church. It was decided to use this to start off the restoration appeal in place at that time.

Colonel Thomlinson died in May 1943 aged 88, after contracting a chill and becoming seriously ill. There was a private funeral at Holy Trinity prior to cremation at Darlington. This was followed by a memorial service at Christ Church in West Hartlepool, conducted by Canon Booth, which enabled people from all areas of public life to pay their respects. A letter was read out from the Bishop of Jarrow, who was sorry he could not attend, but wanted to express *"the great debt which the diocese, as well as the County of Durham, owes to him. It was not only his very ready and active service which he gave with such ability, but also his personal kindliness and generosity to many people, of which I have been increasingly aware during my time in this diocese"*.

Colonel Thomlinson's will included a bequest of £150 to Holy Trinity to set up a Trust Fund, from which the annual interest would be used to pay for the half yearly inspection of the clock and chimes of the church. Any surplus income invested was to be used for any major overhaul and/or renewal of the clock or its chimes. If there was no clock for any reason, such as destruction by war damage, the interest was to be made available to the PCC for religious purposes within Seaton Carew parish.

The Thomlinson window was the last window to be installed in the nave, dedicated on Easter Sunday in 1965. This window is depicted on page 92. It was a gift from Gladys Wainwright in memory of her mother and father. It was designed by Mr Joseph Fisher, A.M.G.P. (1911-82), and fabricated at the workshop of Messrs Shrigley & Hunt, Ltd of Lancaster. Mr Fisher was one of the more significant artists working at this studio after the Second World War. This modern design incorporates many details, including alpha and omega symbols, the iron works that Col. Thomlinson managed, and indeed a depiction of Holy Trinity Church itself, together with representations of different kinds of weather. The order of service for the dedication of the window explains further:

"The Window depicts:

In the beginning God created Heaven and Earth.

The realistic portrayal of the Church and Industry emphasises Reality and our close relationship to God. Man through faith builds, creates and dedicates to the Glory of God.

The Floods and Rainbow signify God's promise to mankind.

Sacrifice, suffering and reward are symbolically represented and set in a triumph of halation and glorification."

At the same time, Mr & Mrs Wainwright gave the Vicars Board, an oak board engraved with a list of vicars. This starts from the time Seaton Carew became a parish in its own right, which is possibly the reason why many local people are not aware that Revd. James Lawson and Revd. Arthur Guinness were the first two clergymen to serve at Holy Trinity.

Kathleen Brooks, the granddaughter of one of the servants of the Thomlinson household, has kindly provided some information about life in the Thomlinson family home. Her grandmother Ada Charlton was born in 1885 and some time before 1912 left her home in Shildon to work for the Thomlinsons at Seaton Hall as a parlour maid. A cook and a nursemaid were also employed. As a result of living at Seaton Hall, she developed a lifelong love of fine china and cutlery.

Ada became indispensible to the household as she cared for Mrs Thomlinson. The family entertained frequently, and General Booth of The

Ada Charlton

Salvation Army was one of their famous visitors. He visited Seaton Hall during a nationwide tour before becoming ill with cancer. Believing the illness to be infectious, Mrs Thomlinson insisted that all the crockery and cutlery that he had used was destroyed, but Ada told her that this was unreasonable and unnecessary.

Despite protestations that the family could not manage without her, Ada married in October 1912 and left to set up her own home in West Hartlepool. This was the same year that Gladys, the Thomlinsons' second daughter and the same age as Ada, married Charles Wainwright. One can only wonder about the contrast between the two weddings. Mrs Thomlinson must have felt some affection for Ada, as she made a gift of a silver hand mirror with an ornate design, which Ada always kept on her dressing table.

CHAPTER 15 – INTO THE 1930S

Revd. George Robinson Cook – vicar 1927 – 1932

George Cook was born in York in 1869 to Thomas and Eliza Cook. His father was a poulterer and hare dealer, born in Stockton, and his mother was born in London. He was educated at St Peter's school in York and Hatfield College in Durham. Mr Cook was a keen athlete, and gained both his Rugby and rowing blues at college.

Revd Cook

He was ordained in 1893 with early appointments at Tudhoe Grange in Spennymoor, Willington, St Paul's West Hartlepool, St Anne's in Ancroft Northumberland, and St Paul's Spennymoor. In 1909 he married Amy Dixon in Durham and came to Seaton Carew in 1927.

Revd. Cook was perhaps more involved with Durham Diocese than many other vicars of Holy Trinity have been. He was an assessor for the diocese, a member of the Diocesan Board of Education, and deanery secretary to the SPG, which was a group with the snappy title of the Society for the Propagation of the Gospel in Foreign Parts (no wonder it was abbreviated for common usage).

It is evident that Revd. Cook threw himself into village life wholeheartedly. He was an excellent chess player, possibly one of the best in the country, and took the role of president of the local chess club. As well as being president of the literary society, he was actively connected with the cricket club and the amateur operatic society. For many years he was chaplain to the Whitworth Lodge of Freemasons and also the Connaught Lodge.

Revd. Cook with the tennis club players

Revd. Cook was a very popular member of the community at Seaton, but he was also well respected in the rest of the town. He was a member of the War Pensions Committee, the Tuberculosis Care Committee, the West Hartlepool Education Committee, and was a governor of Henry Smith School, Hartlepool. One wonders how he found the time to do all this on top of his parish and Diocesan work. It should be noted that there was no curate to help Revd. Cook during this period. He was obviously an example of the old adage: if you want something doing, give it to a busy person.

In 1928 new oak panelling was installed in the chancel, which has lasted well. This cost £75, the funds having been offered by the Seaton Carew War Memorial Committee.

Revd. Cook founded a badminton club in Seaton Carew, which operated from the Temperance Hall. Although very active in community life, he could be rather unforgiving when it came to matters of principle. He was less than impressed when a parishioner placed flowers on the grave of the German Airmen, and gave them a telling off. He was also appalled to see one of the village fish and chip shops opening on a Sunday, and the following week he preached a strong sermon about this. He was insistent that despite the achievements of parishioners in raising money for the new school, they ought to brace themselves for one more effort, to provide an adequate parish hall. The recently vacated school was an ideal candidate for a building to provide this facility.

The centenary of Holy Trinity in 1931 was celebrated with a festival. Special services were held during the anniversary week, with visiting preachers of some note – the Lord Bishop of Durham Dr. Hensley Henson, the Bishop of Jarrow, the Archdeacon of Auckland, Canon R. Poole (vicar of Christ Church and the Rural Dean), and Revd. Cook himself. A sale of work was held, and Colonel Thomlinson, prior to declaring this open, gave an address which consisted of a history of Seaton Carew, which was much appreciated by all present. If only a copy of this had been preserved!

The report in the local newspaper listed the stalls, which bear some resemblance to the type of stalls we still hold today at events: refreshments, cakes, produce, bran tub, and confectionery. There was also a pound stall, a ladies' working party (crafts), Hoopla, and a model Aeroplane stall run by Mr Lancelot Burton and Desmond Burton. They were the grandfather and father of current church member Adrienne Peterson; more is related later about the Burtons, one of the original Seatonian families. The Girl Guides and Girls Friendly Society had their own stalls at this sale of work.

After the sale a whist drive and dance were held, with the newspaper reporting that "*it was evident that the festival spirit was abroad in the land, for all agreed that it was one of the jolliest nights that Seaton had ever had*".

In 1932, a faculty was required for a rather unusual purpose: the removal of a body from the churchyard due to the wrong person having been buried there. The faculty record in Durham University Library fortuitously includes a cutting from a newspaper which further explains this unfortunate affair:

WRONG BODY INTERRED

Seaton Carew Burial Mistake

Echo of Stockton Accident

"*A case of the burial of the wrong body has occurred at Seaton Carew. A young girl named Phyllis Leech, who was injured in a motor cycling accident, died in Stockton Hospital. Her funeral was arranged for Tuesday, and the supposed remains were interred at Seaton Carew churchyard – the coffin having a breastplate bearing her name.*

From something that came to light, inquiries were made, and it has been found that the coffin contains, not the body of Miss Leech, but of an elderly Stockton woman.

Arrangements have been made for the body of Miss Leech to be taken to Seaton Carew today for interment in the churchyard there. A Home Office Order will of course be required for the exhumation of the other coffin.

Mr Leech (the father) described the affair as "terrible and distressing" and adding that he was having a full inquiry made about it."

Revd. Cook took this opportunity to tell the Diocese that the PCC wished there to be no more burials in the churchyard from outside, as there was little room left. They also wanted reassurance that the exhumation would not pose a risk to public health. Before the body could be removed, consent had to be obtained from the Local Medical Officer of Health as well as Seaton Carew's vicar.

The same year, Revd. Cook received some correspondence from the then vicar of Greatham, Austin Rose, relating to the previous arrangement for services to be conducted at Graythorp by the curate of Holy Trinity, Reginald Robson. It seemed that there had been some misunderstanding about the payment of the grant to Seaton Carew for this purpose, and Revd. Rose wanted to sort it out.

However, Revd. Cook became seriously ill in the autumn of this year, and died on 11th December 1932 at Middlesbrough Nursing Home. He was buried at Holy Trinity. The obituary in the Northern Daily Mail recorded that he had been in poor health for some years, and was taken seriously ill two months before his death, spending the last month in a nursing home. The church was completely full for his funeral, with representatives from many of the organisations that he had been involved with during his time at Seaton Carew. The chancel was lined with wreaths and the choir sang "How bright those glorious spirits shine" in leading the procession from the church to the grave.

A new vicar was not appointed immediately, but this did not stop Revd. Rose from pursuing the issue of Graythorp. He wrote to Reginald Robson, terminating the arrangement between the incumbents of Seaton and Greatham for the curate's services in Graythorp. He was careful not to lay blame with Mr Robson: *"It is not you, I or anyone else who is at fault. It is the system. The situation in which the parties concerned – especially yourself – are frequently placed may almost be described as an impossible one. I have regretfully to conclude that the arrangement is not workable."*

Further correspondence in early 1933 shows that Revd. Cook had been keen to continue the Graythorp arrangement. However, the Trustees had not realised that there was a considerable gap between the work paid for through the formal agreement and the level of input they were actually getting in Graythorp. Revd. Rose believed that the promise of a new incumbent at Seaton provided an opportune time to make changes without personal bias. The new vicar would be able to assess the relationship between Graythorp and Seaton Carew and make a decision. Revd. Rose was openly critical of Holy Trinity for not carrying out the work that they were being paid for: *"Seaton Carew has, for some years, had all the benefit of this grant, and Graythorp, for whom it is expressly given, has had very little."* We cannot know whether this was an oversight or whether it was deliberate, but it seems clear that Revd. Rose was not going to get anywhere with this until a new vicar arrived.

Frank Oswald Scott – vicar 1933 – 1935

Frank Oswald Scott was born in 1884 in Newcastle-upon-Tyne. He attended the London College of Divinity then Queen's College Oxford, where he achieved a Theology degree in 1914 and an MA in 1918. In 1909 he was licensed as a stipendiary curate at St Margaret's Church, Ipswich, and moved to Holy Trinity Oxford in 1911 then St Luke's Liverpool in 1915-16. During the war, in 1917, he was named in the London Gazette as one of a number of temporary chaplains to HM Forces.

After periods at Holy Apostle Leicester and St Gabriel in Bishop Wearmouth, Revd. Scott took up the incumbency at Seaton Carew on 22nd June 1933. The Bishop of Durham, Dr Hensley Henson, admitted him to the living at the licensing service.

The Bishop referred to his predecessor Revd. Cook's time at Seaton, saying "You will recall how your old vicar, frequently under the disadvantage of physical weakness, fulfilled a faithful ministry among you". He reflected that they would be looking forward with expectation and hope to Revd. Scott's ministry that would begin among them that night. Mr Scott had been in holy orders for 24 years, 11 of which had been spent in Durham Diocese (at Bishop Wearmouth).

Revd. Scott had been in post less than a week when the indomitable vicar of Greatham, Revd. Rose, wrote to him raising the spectre of the long running dispute over services to Graythorp. Mr Robson the curate must have continued to do some work there, as contrary to the impression given in previous correspondence of it already being stopped, Revd. Rose suggested the current activity should be terminated on Aug 1st. He suggested a break of 6 or 12 months in which Graythorp would manage without any support, for Rev Scott to decide whether to reopen the subject.

The records do not include both sides of subsequent correspondence, but what has survived makes it clear that Rev Scott became quite irritated by Revd. Rose's endless letters, at one point issuing a challenge: "would you, in similar circumstances, have renounced Graythorp, and have expected the Incumbent to make up the financial loss?"

We do not know whether Revd. Scott had the patience of a saint or not, but it was certainly tried, and in the end he lost it. He asked for a straight yes or no as to whether Revd. Rose wanted a clean cut and final severance between Seaton Carew and Graythorp, or whether he wanted a new arrangement. There are no other references to the relationship between the two areas so it is assumed it broke down after this. Eventually, Greatham Church members got their wish and managed to relinquish responsibility for Graythorp in 1963, when it was transferred wholly to the care of Holy Trinity.

Unfortunately Revd. Scott could not live up to the expectations laid out by the Bishop at his admittance to the living of Seaton Carew. He suffered from ill health during his time at Seaton and does not appear to have made as much of a mark as his predecessors. He moved to St Paul's in Hartlepool in December 1935 after only 2 years at Holy Trinity, and stayed there until 1942. The curate Reginald Robson was left to hold the fort for two months after Revd. Scott's departure, until the next vicar was appointed in February 1936.

CHAPTER 16 - STABILITY AND PROGRESS

Reverend James Booth vicar 1936 – 1954

James Booth, later Canon Booth, was born in 1885 in South Shields, to James and Barbara Booth. His father was a marine engineer born in Selby, and his mother was born in South Shields. He was a graduate of Durham University, gaining his first degree in 1909 and was made Deacon in 1910 and ordained in 1911. He served as Curate at Dunston in Wickham, Tyne & Wear, then moved to St John's Darlington. He was a temporary chaplain to the forces in 1915; this was changed to an honorary position in 1919. He was awarded an M.A. in 1920. James married Eva Burnip in 1926 at South Shields.

Canon Booth

In 1924 Revd. Booth became vicar of Jarrow, where he handled the parish carefully during the depression of the 1930s. He gained recognition for this with an appointment as an Honorary Canon of Durham Cathedral. In 1932 he wrote and published a 35-page book, "The Story of the Old Church and Monastery Jarrow", which is described as an interesting history with local adverts from the 1930s.

He came to Seaton Carew in February 1936 and served for 18 years, the third longest serving vicar of Holy Trinity. He was described by Derek Hornby as the classic village parson, who kept his own "village directory" of every household in the village, with notes as to whether they were a churchgoer or not, their jobs and whether a home visit was necessary. When Derek asked for a reference for an application to Bede College, Revd. Booth simply opened the file, announced he did not need any further information, and asked him to return in an hour. At the appointed time, Derek turned up and was handed the story of his life in about 500 words.

One notable effort during his incumbency at Seaton was the establishment of the new mission church at Owton Manor, St James, part of Seaton parish at that time, which was much needed due to a rapid increase in house building in that area. The PCC records from this time show a steady and determined effort to raise funds and set up the church.

Although Revd. Booth believed passionately in the church and was assiduous in making sure everything went on smoothly, he had a fatal flaw which would not have gone down well with today's congregations: his sermons lasted over half an hour. He was a keen theologian and spent a long time preparing them, but it is safe to say that they were far beyond the understanding of most of the congregation.

However, some relief was obtained during Lent. Revd. Booth thought Holy Trinity was the most beautiful of any churches that he knew, and therefore to practice the abstinence and denial that he preached, he denied himself the use of his own church, bringing in other clergymen to preach. This was a great sacrifice for the vicar, but the choir boys (and most certainly the congregation as well) were delighted, for the visiting clergy's sermons were a lot shorter.

As with his predecessors, Revd. Booth continued to make improvements to the church. The altar rails which are currently in place at Holy Trinity were installed in 1939 at a cost of £50, along with a priest's stall in the south west corner of the nave (also £50), both of which were from private subscriptions, a motor driven organ blower to the organ (£48), new electric lighting (£70), and replacement of the old painted pitch pine choir stalls with oak stalls (£150).

There was some debate among the Diocesan officers who awarded faculties as to whether the altar rails should be approved or not, due to the inclusion of gates in the centre. Revd. Booth's explanation must have been accepted, as they are present today:

"We much prefer to have them as we have both aged and blind people who come regularly to their communion and the absence of such gates would be an inconvenience and perhaps a danger. The present rail is very shaky and I often notice the difficulty infirm people have in rising from their knees even with its support. Another reason why we prefer the gates is that in the holiday season a large number of visitors come into the church and it is really desirable to close the sanctuary."

Revd. Booth was a gentle man, kind and understanding, and never happier than when distributing the annual church gifts from bequests to selected parishioners. Not only did he work hard for Holy Trinity, but he also assisted the West Hartlepool Education Committee in producing the first Religious Instruction Syllabus.

However, he could be forceful when principles were at stake. He joined other clergymen in the area in a protest against the proposal to open the amusements on a Sunday.

It was during Canon Booth's time that a memorial was erected for the people of Seaton Carew who died in the Second World War. The names recorded on this plaque are as follows:

Denis Clark	John Frederick Hodgson	John Robert Pegg
Ralph Cole	Robert Henry Holmes	Margaret Welton Pickering
Gilbert Danie	George Ingledew	Herbert Richardson
Douglas Croft Elliott	John Johnson	Andrew Ridpath
George Ennis	Eric Liddle	Edward Michael Shepherd
Albert Fletcher	Harold Lucas	Arthur Waller
Joseph Kenneth Forster	George Edward Markwell	Eric Waller
Thomas Greener	Denis McKay	John Robert Waller
Harry Hood Hannah	Harold Myers	William Norman Welsh
William Harker	Frederick William Neesam	John Robert Whitley

On 19th September 1954, Canon Booth finished the 8 am service and complained of feeling unwell. He returned to the vicarage, where he died almost immediately of a heart attack.

Canon Booth's wife presented an Oak Credence Table to Holy Trinity in memory of her husband, which is still used at every communion service.

Booth memorial table

Family memorials at the time of Revd. Booth

Thomas Williams

A brass plaque on the south wall of the nave remembers Thomas Williams, fondly remembered by those he supervised in his job as well as by his family:

"In Memory of
Thomas Williams
Works Manager at the West Hartlepool Steelworks
Who died 18th July 1936
Erected as a tribute by his Workmen & Staff"

Thomas Williams was born in 1869 in Treforest, Wales, the youngest of six children born to John and Elizabeth Williams. His father worked in the iron works eventually as a foreman, and most of the children were born at Glamorgan. By 1871 the family had moved to Stockton. At the age of 16 Thomas was a stocktaker at the old Moor works at Stockton, and gradually worked his way up to become manager there. Thomas married Ann Hutchinson in 1893.

Thomas and Ann Williams

In 1901 they were living on The Green at Seaton Carew. The family later moved to a house on The Cliff, which they named Gwalia. This is an archaic Welsh name for Wales, a reference to the land of Thomas' birth. It is now the Rothbury Guest House, on the corner of The Cliff and Queen Street. Thomas and Ann had three sons and four daughters.

Thomas moved to the South Durham Steelworks as manager in 1899, and retained that position for 33 years, retiring in 1932. On his retirement presentations were made to him by the directors, officials, and staff of the steelworks and also by the workmen. The tributes indicated that he was much appreciated not only for his work, but also as a considerate manager who had always been ready to help the workforce their sports, entertainments, and amusements. Although the steel trade was suffering acutely from the industrial depression of the 1930s, Thomas Williams and the other managers expressed confidence that there would be an improvement soon.

The Williams family c. 1912

Mr Williams, like other Seaton residents noted in this book, was a community leader who supported many of the local efforts during the war. He was a member of the War Memorial Committee, the Teesside Lodge of Freemasons, and took an active interest in work for the blind. At one time he was treasurer of the Hartlepool Liberal Association.

Thomas' principal hobby was music. When at Stockton, he acted as chapel organist at Portrack, and, after coming to Seaton, he was an enthusiastic supporter of movements to encourage the study of music and took an active part in the work of organizing various festivals. His obituary noted that he was prominently associated with Holy Trinity Church, Seaton Carew.

Thomas had heart trouble for a number of years and passed away in 1936 at the age of 71. The church was full for his funeral service at Holy Trinity, including many former colleagues, staff from other firms in the district and a large number of Mr Williams' personal friends. Canon Booth conducted a fully choral service.

William Henry Loveridge

The set of Thompson furniture was begun with the installation of a carved oak vicar's stall with prayer desk, said to be designed with Rev Booth's rather large proportions in mind! This was placed in the church in 1939, the gift of Mr W.E. Loveridge in memory of his father the late W.H. Loveridge. It is the earliest piece of furniture in Holy Trinity from the workshop of Robert Thompson of Kilburn, known as "Mousey Thompson" because of his trademark mouse carvings.

William Henry Loveridge was born in 1857, another Welshman who moved to the north east of England. In 1881 he was living at Front Street, Seaton Carew, with his sister Edith. He married Anna Maria Oughtred in 1883 in Hartlepool; she was the daughter of a corn, seed and grain merchant, William Oughtred from Stockton. The family lived in Seaton Carew at a large detached house on the Front named Langton and also at a house named Ivy Croft. They had two daughters, Eva and Edith Winifred Loveridge, and two sons, William Edmonds and Henry Norris Loveridge.

William Henry was recorded as an iron merchant in the 1911 census. He died in 1938.

Vicar's chair and prayer desk; a Mousey Thompson piece

CHAPTER 17 – MORE RECENT HISTORY OF HOLY TRINITY

The main focus of this book is on the early history of Holy Trinity. Without substantial research most of this is not generally available to the ordinary member of the public, whereas the period after Revd. Booth's time is more accessible through memories of the current parishioners.

The remainder of the story therefore consists of pen portraits of the remaining vicars and some examples of memorials and information provided by parishioners from recent times. One day someone else may take up the mantle and write another volume to cover the later period.

Canon Joseph Maughan – vicar 1955-1962

Joseph Maughan was born in 1911 and graduated from St John's College Durham in 1930. He married Agnes Waugh in Newcastle in 1932. After taking up the post of vicar of St Aidan's in West Hartlepool in 1931, which he held for four years, he was appointed to Durham St Cuthbert in 1935, then moved to Jarrow St Paul. He became vicar of Seaton Carew in May 1955.

Revd Maughan

One of the first things Revd. Maughan did was to make alterations to improve the vicarage. Instead of embarking on a fund raising drive, the church applied for a counterpart mortgage, a device to secure a loan that was borrowed from the Church Commissioners over a term of 15 years, with interest charged at around £11 per annum. Other items of expenditure included a choir trip (£11) and the Diocesan quota, which in those days was only £91 – if only that were the case today. The sale of work raised an impressive £351. If we needed our coffee mornings to raise a similar multiplier of 3.8 times today's parish share payment to the Diocese, each one would have to raise nearly £108,000! This probably says more about the Diocesan budget than about the parish church's fund raising history.

Early in his incumbency, Revd. Maughan became involved in supporting the project to build a temporary church in Rossmere Way at Owton Manor, begun by Canon Booth. A Miss Susannah Bell had left a legacy for this purpose, with a condition that the church building had to be started within six months of her death. A request for funding to the Church Commissioners was successful, raising £23,000.

The foundation stone for the new church was laid in 1957 and Rev H P Johnston was appointed as Curate there. The dedication of St James' Church Owton Manor by the Bishop of Durham took place on September 17th 1958. A fund for a parsonage house at Owton Manor was set up, with a target of £6000. By 1960 preparations started to be made for St James to become an independent church.

Within two years of his arrival at Seaton, Revd. Maughan was able to report that the number of communicants and the collections at Holy Trinity were both at record levels. Particularly pleasing was the increase in the number of young people attending. Even though the Owton Manor project must have taken a considerable amount of Revd. Maughan's time, he did not neglect his home church; he organised repairs to the clock and organ and arranged for the installation of a new boiler in Holy Trinity, as well as repairs to the vicarage. The vicar was assisted by curates Ernest Sidebottom (1954-1956) and Herbert Johnson (1957-1961).

The accounts show that in 1959 instead of a choir outing, the PCC gave a contribution towards a camp at Staithes. PCC minutes record that Revd. Maughan asked the Education Authority for a school hall to be built, but was refused as they had committed their funding and in any case only wanted to support the provision of new classrooms.

Revd. Maughan left Holy Trinity in 1962 to go to St Helen's in Kelloe, but first kindly arranged for the vicarage to be decorated ready for his successor. In his parting address to the PCC, the vicar noted that the problem of Owton Manor had been solved, but there was a great deal to do in the parish of Seaton Carew, as the population was increasing. The parishioners made a collection and gave Revd. Maughan £50 as a leaving gift.

Revd. Maughan died in 1986 aged 75, at Newcastle upon Tyne.

Cecil Charles Greenwood vicar 1962-1972

Cecil Greenwood was born in around 1900 and like many clergymen was an Oxford graduate (1921), with an M.A. awarded in 1923. He became curate at Blackburn then Mossley Hill in Liverpool, and moved to Yorkshire in 1931 for his first appointment as a vicar. He served in the Ripon area then moved to Harrogate.

Revd Greenwood

He arrived in Seaton Carew in August 1962 and immediately turned his attention to the introduction of activities to develop the life of the parish. These included the formation of a church fellowship for men and women over the age of 18, involving film shows and visiting speakers on topics of interest. Mr Hauxwell and Mr Kirk had volunteered to help with a youth club, and Messrs Joyson, Collingwood, Forster, Modrel & Lithgo had agreed to run Teenage Dances fortnightly for young people aged 13-19 who were connected with the church.

Revd. Greenwood also proposed the reopening of the Sunday School and Guide Company. A sub committee was then appointed to consider the enlargement of the parish magazine, with 350 subscriptions being achieved in the following year. The parish had a pilgrimage to Iona, and a Parish Christmas party and Shrove Tuesday social were held. The parishioners must have experienced quite a whirlwind of activity.

The parish hall was well used, by Infant Welfare, the Gardeners Society (summer and autumn shows and committee meetings), receptions, whist drives, and the Townswomen's Guild Handicrafts group. A restoration appeal was set up with target of £2000 for church fabric; the north wall needed particular attention, a new roof was also needed and electric lights were to be installed. The verger Norman Lithgo completed 25 years of service, and a collection was organised for him.

The attention to parish activities certainly paid dividends; the youth club doubled in membership from 20 to 40, and had to be split into a junior and a senior section. The Sunday School had 89 children on its books between the ages of 5 and 14. In 1963 permission was obtained to enlarge the primary school by adding two classrooms, making it into a one form entry school for 280 children. It was during Revd. Greenwood's time that the bodies of the German airmen were removed from Holy Trinity churchyard and reinterred at Cannock Chase.

Revd. Greenwood obtained a loan of £1000 repayable over five years from the Diocese for the repairs to the church. The letter awarding the loan asks him not to say too much about the loan to other incumbents and parishes, because they had a limited amount available and did not want to set off a rush of applications. A nod and a wink approach would not work nowadays – the effort involved in grant and loan applications is quite staggering.

In the mid-1960s there were some proposals to unite the Church of England and the Methodist church. This ran into serious opposition throughout the country. Parish records show that Holy Trinity PCC members were not exactly in favour. A motion that the "PCC welcomes with joy" the recent decision to press ahead with the proposals was amended to "notes with interest"!

An indication of some of the trends of the time came with a request for a Tupperware stall to be included in the Sale of Work, with 10% of the takings to go to the church. A proposal was also made in 1967 to allow girls into the church choir, and after consulting other church members, the vicar agreed, as long as they attended practices on Thursday evenings. Volunteers called "Pivoteers" visited all the newcomers to welcome them to the parish, as a result of the rapid growth in housing in Seaton. An extension to the school was also built.

John Edward Scott vicar 1974-1974

Rev JE Scott

John Scott was born in Birmingham in 1928 and initially trained as a civil engineer. He married Beryl May Burrows in 1951 and they adopted two children, Stephen and Catriona. He decided to change career and attended Worcester Ordination College in 1966-68 before taking up the post of curate at Llandudno in 1968 then at Winshill in Staffordshire in 1970. He came to Seaton Carew in July 1973 but only served here until October 1974.

Revd. Scott seems to have had a gap after leaving Seaton, as he did not take up his next incumbency until 1977, at Ellistown in Leicestershire. The answer may be that he was writing a book with his wife Beryl, entitled "Lord How Long?" which looked at the purpose of suffering and its meaning. He left Ellistown in 1983, moving to Raveningham in Norfolk then settling in Lenzie in Dumbartonshire, Scotland. He was chaplain to two hospitals, a prison and a primary school there.

He must have felt an affinity with Scotland while at Seaton, because if you look carefully at the photograph of Revd. Scott you can just make out some tartan. Some remember him walking round wearing a kilt, which was a brave thing to do in Seaton, with the freezing cold wind coming straight off the North Sea! He is also remembered as having a Morris Minor car.

At his first PCC meeting, Revd Scott set out his Spiritual Strategy for the parish, based on his belief that the family was important and that family worship was an essential part of church life. His plans for services may have been quite difficult to follow, with different Sundays in the month being nominated as a children's service, and with children being moved between the Sunday School and the church service at different times. He initiated the Wednesday morning service for the school, and started the tradition of lay people administering the chalice at Holy Communion.

During Revd. Scott's time, there were concerns that the church hall was losing money, and some organisations which used it moved to the new Seaton Youth Centre. It was suggested the hall be abandoned, and attempts were made to find a buyer for it, but these were unsuccessful. Similarly, the vicarage was in a poor condition and the Diocese could not be persuaded to help. However, it deteriorated to such an extent that when the Bishop of Durham visited, he recommended urgent action and it was agreed that it should be demolished when a new parsonage house was completed, and the land turned into a car park.

In an attempt to vary worship and meetings, the vicar asked if the parish would buy a projector and films to use in church and with the guild, Sunday school and the day school. It appears the PCC were less than impressed at this suggestion; they decided that Revd. Scott should buy them, sending the clear message that they were clearly his responsibility, and suggested that he could hire them to the parish on the occasions when needed.

The church records give a sense that there was some discomfort at the speed of the changes brought about by Revd. Scott. This has been confirmed by current parishioners who remember these times. When he suggested removing some pews to relieve the shortage of space at the back of the church, the PCC minutes record that this led to "a wide-ranging discussion on change and stability, particularly in the conduct of the services". The PCC members insisted that the members of the congregation who usually sat in these pews should be consulted, and that two pews in the centre should be removed and one turned round, but as a temporary arrangement only. The People's Warden Mr Simmons resigned in July 1974 and was replaced by Brian Lithgo.

Revd. Scott did not stay long at Seaton; he left in September 1974. This plunged Holy Trinity into a two-year interregnum, the longest in its history. Part of the problem was the lack of a vicarage, and there were discussions with the Bishop about this; the dilemma was whether a new vicarage should be purpose-built, or a small house be purchased.

The retired Canon Shepherd came to the rescue and led services during this time, but the real hero was George Holmes, who chaired the PCC and made sure that the right decisions were taken; he regularly chased the Diocese for a new incumbent. The minutes during this period regularly display George's dry sense of humour and firm determination to defend Holy Trinity against anyone who tried to force the church members to do anything against their wishes. There was a keen interest in making sure the next vicar was carefully selected, and the state of affairs certainly provided a good canvas for the next vicar to make his mark.

William Worley vicar 1976-2003

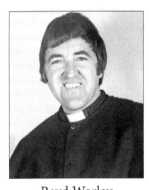

Revd Worley

William Worley was born in Low Fell, Gateshead in 1937. His father was a carpenter. Before entering ministry, Bill worked in commerce and shipping, and completed his military service for the Royal Air Force. He studied at Cranmer Hall of St John's College, Durham University between 1969 and 1972, gaining his full colours as a sportsman, not in rugby as those who know him might expect, but in football. He did however play rugby for a senior county club, Gateshead Fell.

Bill became Curate of Consett in 1972 and served for four years, three of which were under Revd. Derek Hodgson, who later became Archdeacon of Auckland then Durham. Revd. Hodgson left Consett in 1975, leaving Bill to run the parish on his own. He was invited by the Bishop of Durham to consider the parish of Seaton Carew in 1976. Bill relates that he and his wife came to look at the church, and had an overwhelming sense that this was the right place for them. Their fate was sealed when Mary said to Bill "I don't know about you, but I'm coming here!" Holy Trinity had made a welcoming impression, as it often seems to have done.

This began a long and happy incumbency of 27 years, second only to John Lawson's length of service. The new vicar's first instinct was to roll up his sleeves and tackle the physical state of the churchyard. This was a good idea, as a churchyard is often regarded as an outward sign of whether a church is loved and cared for or not. At the time of the Worleys' arrival, the churchyard was occupied by ponies, which were eating the flowers among the graves. The only thing to do was to go out and buy a grass cutter and get started.

As Bill and Mary settled in, it became apparent that there was a lot of work needed on the church building as well, and they embarked on a major restoration programme. The finials on the tower were cracked, and showing signs of movement, so they had to be reduced and capped for safety's sake. The crumbling north wall and chancel wall were repaired and attention paid to the bottom section of the other walls, at a cost of £33,000. The chancel was re-roofed, pews stripped and lightened, and carpets were laid in the chancel, sanctuary and aisles. As already mentioned, the windows in the south wall of the chancel were replaced using the original medallions. A new heating system was installed, and the old boiler house, which regularly flooded, was filled in with concrete.

During this time, under the guidance of Revd. Worley, the PCC decided to buy the church hall, and undertook a modernisation programme to make it more usable. The oldest part of it, which used to be the National School, was sold for a sheltered housing scheme. New toilets, a kitchen, and a garden store room were added, and the ancient gas heaters, suspended from the ceiling, were removed from the hall and a lower ceiling with modern lighting was installed.

Bill's wife Mary Worley was a qualified parish worker, and had experience as a licenced worker in the East End of London at Walthamstow. They had met at Durham University, where they were both students at Cranmer Hall. Although she did not wish to be ordained, Mary made just as much of a contribution to parish life at Seaton Carew as if she had been. She had the idea of introducing a church-based group for young people, based on a model she had seen at Walthamstow. The Adventurers groups were born, Mary leading the group for 5-7 year olds, and Bill leading one for those over 7 years old. When Alan Brown joined the church, an inimitable team was formed and so many young people had a great time, that waiting lists had to be set up. Mary succeeded Rosa Bulmer as PCC secretary and served in this capacity for many years, as well as providing secretarial support to her husband.

Almost as soon as Revd. Worley arrived at Seaton, Canon Bullock took him to the church school and introduced him as the next Chair of Governors. Bill complied and carried out the role between 1977 and 1993. His devotion was demonstrated among other things by accompanying the school to Carlton Camp not once, but twice.

While Revd. Worley inherited the Wednesday morning service for the school, he loved having this chance to talk to the children in church as well as through his regular visits to the school, and gained a glowing reference in an Ofsted report. Many children were brought for confirmation during his time at Seaton Carew. He also introduced the Christingle service, an idea he brought from Consett but reinvigorated it by holding it on Christmas Eve. This is still a hugely popular tradition, which over the years has raised a substantial amount for the Children's Society. For many families, Christmas would not be the same if they did not attend the Christingle service.

Revd. Worley also took up the position of Chairman of Seaton Cricket Club after Derek Hornby's untimely death in 1987, continuing up until 2002. Locals soon got used to seeing a clergyman as a regular at the bar, proving that mission can happen anywhere. Bill's secret was undoubtedly his down to earth approach, far removed from some of the earlier vicars whose experience was somewhat distant from that of the average church member.

In 1977 the Royal Army Chaplains Department, aware that Revd. Worley was an ex-serviceman, approached him to be an Army Chaplain with the Territorial Army. He carried out this role for 18 years, and was awarded the Territorial Decoration (Queen's Award) for his lengthy service. This sometimes entailed going off to camp, but this was always done using his holidays, to ensure that the parish did not lose out.

A notable event during Bill's incumbency was the celebration of the church's 150th anniversary in 1981-2. This included a visit by the Archbishop of Canterbury, Michael Ramsey, and an exhibition was put together including old photographs, documents, and the Lithgo family tree.

It was only when Bill and Mary retired that church members realised the hard work this superb man and wife team had undertaken. A lot of people willingly took on different jobs to keep things running smoothly. It is at times like this that the true community spirit emerges, reflecting the way in which our predecessors pulled together to support the vicar. The congregation was particularly grateful to Revd. Peter Townsend, who regularly took services, and other clergy, either from other parishes in Hartlepool or those who were retired. Mercifully the interregnum was relatively short, and God sent us just the right minister to take the church forward.

Paul Timothy Allinson – vicar 2004 to date

Paul Timothy Allinson was born in Shipston-on-Stour, near Stratford-upon-Avon, in 1963 to Elizabeth & Walter Allinson. He grew up in Redcar as the seventh of nine children. He was commissioned as a Church Army Officer and evangelist in 1985, ordained deacon in 1991 and priest in 1992 in Durham Cathedral.

Revd Allinson

He became vicar in 2004 and has overseen the renewal of the church building and parish centre, the developments of a Sunday School and new initiatives in music and liturgy. He is also the vicar of Saint John the Baptist Greatham and Chaplain to the Hospital of God Greatham in addition to his incumbency at Seaton Carew. The restoration of our church is a highly significant goal for him and he is determined to see this project to fruition.

Father Paul brings a host of talents to Holy Trinity, not least of which are his energy, enthusiasm, sense of fun, a caring nature and an accessible way of explaining God's word. He is not afraid to don fancy dress at our summer fayres, and joins in heartily in our social events. His expertise from his previous role as Diocesan Children's Adviser has stood him in good stead in serving the schools at Seaton, Greatham and Golden Flatts. Under his guidance the church is thriving, and we have great hopes for the future. The next chapter of the church's history is taking shape.

CHAPTER 18 - NOTABLE FAMILIES AND MEMORIALS OF THE 20TH CENTURY

Stanley Dryden Robinson

Stanley Robinson

Stanley Robinson was born in Seaton Carew in 1909 to Thomas Buick Robinson and Laura Dryden. He was a choirboy and a churchwarden. He had a bad experience in the Second World War as a prisoner of war, captured by the Japanese on the surrender of Singapore. He relied on his Christian faith to survive in the POW camps.

On his death, Mr Robinson left a generous legacy to establish a trust fund. He also provided choir pews, a bishop's chair and the altar rail, all produced by the "Mousey" Thompson workshop at Kilburn, well known for the carvings of mice incorporated into the design. This symbolises industry in quiet places. Holy Trinity's is one of the finest collections of this craftsman's work in the Diocese of Durham. The Thompson workshop still exists, and visitors can watch the furniture being created.

 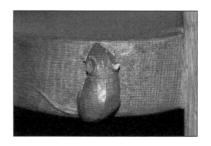

Thompson mice on altar rail (left) and choir stalls (right)

The choir stalls can be seen in the Thompson workshop in this photograph:

Choir pews

There is a small plaque on the inside of the front choir pew on the south side, with the following inscription:

> *"To the glory of God, and in loving memory of*
> *Stanley Dryden Robinson, died 4th March 1970.*
> *Choir boy and Churchwarden."*

PCC minutes from this time showed some tensions between the church and the Diocesan Advisory Committee (DAC) who made decisions about changes to furniture and fittings. The Committee stipulated that there should only be 4 choir stalls and two benches for the chancel, no longer than 12 feet and movable. They considered that this would give a larger area in front of the Communion rail, so that if at any time the church wished to put the altar in the nave, it could be moved. The PCC minutes say that church members "agreed to the first part, but regarded the second suggestion as a piece of impertinence".

There was also an argument over the plaque. The DAC did not want to allow "To the glory of God", but the PCC felt this was a most un-Christian suggestion. They got their own way in this, but lost out on their wish to place the inscription on the end of the choir stall facing the Communion rail, where it could be read by visitors. It was placed on the inside and is therefore only visible to the choir members.

Stanley Robinson also gave two fine churchwardens' wands, which were dedicated at a family communion service in 1964.

Wands held by current
churchwardens
Jackie Hamilton and Alan Brown

The Clark family

A Sanctuary Chair on the north side of the church was presented by Mr W. Wilson Clark and family, in memory of his wife Annie Clark. This carved oak chair, given in 1948, is another piece by Thompson of Kilburn. The inscription is not easy to spot, because it is at the base of the chair back, partially hidden by the red cushion. It reads:

"In Grateful Memory of a Loving Wife and Mother
Annie, Wife of William Wilson Clark
Whitsunday 1948."

Sanctuary chair by
Mousey Thompson

William Wilson Clark was born in 1871 in Hartlepool, to parents William and Jane Clark. He was a school master at Ward Jackson Junior School. He married Annie Sherwood in 1897 at Thirsk and they had 7 children.

Since the mid-1920s, Wilson Clark had taken children from Ward Jackson camping in the Cleveland Hills. However, in 1929 he was told that the field they usually used at Pinchinthorpe near Roseberry Topping would no longer be available, so he went hunting for a new site. One day he cycled to Carlton-in-Cleveland where he used to spend some of his summer holidays, and while making enquiries, was directed to the vicar

William Wilson Clark

Canon Kyle, who had bought the field on which the church school had been built. Canon Kyle offered the surplus land to Wilson Clark for £250.

On returning to Hartlepool, Wilson Clark approached the Mayor of the town, George Turnbull, who agreed to help raise funds to buy the field. A charity was formed and the citizens of Hartlepool contributed to it. On 20th October 1931, the field was bought and signed for by Wilson Clark and two other "trustees". Carlton Camp was born, dedicated for all time to the use of the children of West Hartlepool. Accommodation blocks were built later. Thanks are due to Hartlepool Council for this information, found on the Carlton Centre website.

Across the years, hundreds of children from Holy Trinity Primary School have had an amazing time at Carlton Camp (now Carlton Outdoor Centre), so it is somewhat fitting to know that there is a link between Holy Trinity Church and the centre's founder.

Hilda Chaila née Lightfoot

Hilda Chaila donated a bible to Holy Trinity church. She was the daughter of Alfred Henry Lightfoot and Mary Ann (neé Westgarth), who were married at Holy Trinity in 1900.

Hilda was born in 1907 in old Hartlepool, with a twin brother Thomas. The early death of her father resulted in her moving to London, where she, her mother and two sisters worked as receptionists in a well known hotel. It was here that she met and married a French business man named Jules Chaila, before moving to Paris to live.

Wedding of Alfred and Mary Ann Lightfoot

Hilda was visiting her twin brother's family in Hartlepool during 1939 when it became obvious that war was to break out. Hurriedly she returned to France and remained there throughout the war, out of contact with her English family for the whole of that period. It was only after her return at the end of the war that she was able to relate her experiences.

Somehow Hilda had managed to disguise her English nationality from the Germans during their occupation of France. Involved in some clandestine work in Paris, she and her husband were warned by someone in a park not to go back to their flat, as it was to be subjected to a search. This resulted in them travelling to Marseilles where the German occupation was less intense. They remained there until the end of the war. During this time she helped in the repatriation of escaped British airmen. For this she received a letter of thanks from the Red Cross Association.

On the death of her husband in 1959, Hilda continued to live in Marseilles and earned a living by teaching, and sometimes broadcasting, lessons on the English language. Her strong religious faith resulted in her obtaining a licence to become a lay preacher at her church in Marseilles.

Most summers during the 1960s, 1970s and 1980s she left the heat of Marseilles and spent part of the time with her twin brother and his family in the town and the rest in the Staincliffe Hotel. Attending the church regularly, she donated a bible in memory of her mother. During this time she became special friends of Rev Bill Worley and his wife Mary. Her mother Mary lived at Glencliffe on The Cliff in Seaton Carew and died in 1962.

As old age approached, Hilda's visits to England were curtailed and eventually she put herself in the hands of the church, and spent the remainder of her life in a nursing home, run by Nuns named the "Sisters of the Poor".

Hilda died on February 6th 2000. She is buried with her husband in St Peter's cemetery, Marseilles.

George Holmes

George Holmes was a much respected member of Holy Trinity and he and his wife Mrs Edna Holmes worked extremely hard on behalf of the parish, with good humour and a quiet sense of fun. George is remembered by the gift of hymn boards, a wooden box for hymn numbers, and a candle snuffer. His widow Mrs Edna Holmes has kindly provided the following information:

"By the time he died in June 2000 aged 80, my husband George Holmes, a shy unassuming man, had held various posts and done various jobs in the service of Holy Trinity Church.

The Reverend Bill Worley who was Vicar at the time wrote the following appreciation of him in the parish magazine just after his death:

"It is only a few months ago at the Annual General Meeting of the PCC that George gave us a year's notice of his standing down as Vice Chairman of the PCC. His death on June 4th was never expected.

George was from Liverpool and came to Seaton via Magdalen College Oxford, Gordonstoun School where he was classics master, and Henry Smith Grammar School where he remained until retirement.

No church can function without the contributions of the laity and George's contribution was enormous; Vice Chairman going on 30 years, Treasurer 37 years, and this last 23 years adviser, confidant and much revered friend of the current Vicar.

During the early 1970s, when the parish experienced two periods of interregnum, it was George who, although in full time employment, nevertheless guided the parish through and at times also covered the positions of organist, magazine editor and printer, and general factotum.

When it is also considered that he was a member of Hartlepool Deanery Synod for at least a quarter of a century, a member of the Durham Diocesan Board of Finance and a member of the Bishop of Durham's Council, his overall contribution to the Anglican Church in this area was enormous."

George's last big job for the Diocese was in 1983/84 as chairman and organiser of Assessors for the Potential Income of <u>all</u> the parishes in the Diocese of Durham (it is now known as Parish Share). It was a job that he carried out conscientiously and as fairly as possible, with only the aid of fifteen assessors, a portable typewriter and a telephone, and there are a lot of parishes in the Diocese. It was not a pleasant task, as not everybody likes a tax gatherer."

Edna Holmes and Freda Robinson at the Garden Party 1972

Mrs Edna Holmes has herself been a stalwart of Holy Trinity for many years, as a member of the PCC and an active supporter of a wide range of activities. She and George are excellent examples of people who have taken Holy Trinity to their hearts and served faithfully.

The Burton family

Barry and Adrienne Peterson and Cheryl Burton gave the oak bookcase which holds the hymnbooks at Holy Trinity Church, in memory of her mother and father, Sylvia (née Swain) and Lancelot Desmond (Des) Burton. The family also gave a silver jug in memory of Freda Swain, Sylvia's sister.

Burtons are shown living in Seaton Carew in the earliest records, and as with the Lithgos and Bulmers, direct descendants still live here. For many generations, the Burton family were the village builders, living in and working from 9 Green Terrace. This cottage is reputed to be the oldest in the village, and still stands today, having been sympathetically restored about 30 years ago.

The last in the line of village builders was Rowland Burton (Rowley). In many small communities, the local builder was often also the village undertaker, but not in this case. There is no record of who the undertaker was, but perhaps it was the village joiner or carpenter. However, in the 1950s, Rowley was occasionally engaged to build brick lining walls for new graves in the churchyard. Members of the family can remember him calling them 'proper graves', giving the impression that the practice was quite common in pre WW2 days. It is suspected that this developed because the Victorians had a nasty habit of re-using graves, without much regard to the existing occupant. Brick lining and a heavy flat stone on top would certainly deter such practices.

There seems to have been a tradition of naming the eldest Burton either Richard or Richard William. Both Rowley's father and grandfather were given this name, as were his son and grandson. The name Burton is derived from the Anglo-Saxon name for a lowland farmer, although this does not seem to fit with generations of builders.

The 1894 Whelan's Directory of County Durham shows that Rowley's father Richard Burton (who was born in 1872) was working as a builder from Green Terrace. Richard was the eldest of seven sons born to Richard senior (1850 – 1921) and his wife Ellen (née Parker born 1851): Richard, Rupert, Wilfred, Horace, Lancelot, Percy and Edgar.

Lancelot provides the direct line down to current church member Adrienne Peterson (née Burton) and her sister Cheryl: he was their grandfather, having married Edith Mary Burton. Normally when researching family trees, one looks for the mother's maiden name; however, in this case Edith was already a Burton, daughter of Charles and Mary Ann Burton.

Charles and Mary Ann had four children, William, Charles, Miriam (Minnie) and Edith. Charles senior was a florist, working from Seaton Gardens, between Proctor's Court and the farmyard. Today this is part of Seaton Carew Park, between Seaton Music shop and the car park, off Station Lane.

However, Charles was not born in Seaton; he came here from East Dereham in Norfolk during the late Victorian boom years of trade and industry in West Hartlepool. The new middle class merchants and associated professionals were rich, and they aspired to the lifestyle of the upper classes. Charles Burton provided floral decoration for balls and other social events. His son Charles was a portrait painter, and he too provided a service to the new aspirational classes.

Lance Burton and Edie Burton married in 1914; it is not often that a woman moves 200 miles, then marries an unrelated man with the same surname. They spent almost all of their married life living in Victoria Street, where they bred champion Pomeranians and Dandie Dinmont terriers. The following photograph shows the wedding party outside Charles' home in Proctors Court.

Burton wedding

The photograph below shows Edie and their nine year old son Des on the beach in 1930, next to a buoy near the newly wrecked vessel, the *Doris*.

Des and Edie Burton

Life as a growing lad in Seaton between between the wars seems to have been idyllic, despite the Depression. Rowley was apprenticed to his father, while Des secured an electrical engineering apprenticeship at Richardson Westgarth. The cousins built a sand yacht, which was based on an Austin Seven chassis. They turned it round, butting the steering wheels at the back, so that it could be steered with a tiller, and rigged it as a gaff cutter complete with bowsprit.

They quickly found that it could be unstable at speed, so they doubled its width at the back. This made it much more stable, and they delighted in telling tales of how the sand yacht went much faster than the old Austin it was based on. They kept it in the yard at Green Terrace, during the days of the trolley buses running along the front. The mast was much higher than the trolley wires, so the mast had to be lowered to get underneath. As time went by, the two boys became very skilled at lowering the mast just enough to get under the wires while still on the move.

Of course the inevitable happened. Early one Sunday morning, before the buses were running, they mistimed the mast lowering and brought down the wires. They decided that the best option was to keep going, and sailed it up Station Lane, turned right into Victoria Street and back into the builder's yard. It didn't go out for the next few weeks until the dust settled! Soon afterwards Rowley and Des had some kind of argument about the sand yacht, and Rowley cut it in two so they each had their own half. Des next developed a passion for building and driving small fast powerboats, which has been passed on to the current generations.

Barton/Framingham families

Members of the Barton and Framingham families have supported Holy Trinity in a variety of ways. While this has included key posts, including secretary to the PCC and assistant treasurer (Diane Barton), and Head Chorister (Sarah Barton), they have also made a notable contribution over many years in fund raising and helping to organise and run social events. Diane, Walter and Sarah Barton, Carol and James Bullock and their families have brought a lot of energy and organisational skills to the church.

This family has also given memorials which are used regularly in church.

Mary Framingham, Diane and Carol's mother, donated the lectionary book from which the reading is given every week in church, in memory of Charles Victor Framingham, her husband. Charles was born in West Hartlepool on

4th February 1933 to Charles and Ruth Framingham and was the eldest of two children. His sister Joyce died in early childhood. Charles was an altar boy, together with David Webster who became a vicar in Hartlepool, at St James' Church. When he left school, he went to work at Siemens as a test equipment service engineer but was made redundant at the age of 57. He married Mary and had three girls, Diane, Carol and Hazel and the family moved to Seaton Carew in 1967. The girls attended Golden Flatts School.

Charles loved taking the family on holiday and would travel all over the country during the school holidays. He used to keep diaries of all the miles they travelled and how much petrol he put in the car. Charles especially loved the Christmas services at Holy Trinity when he joined his grandchildren Sarah, Adam and Daniel. Charles died at home twelve days after celebrating the new millennium with his family at Center Parcs.

Rita Barton, Walter's mother, donated the Paschal and Advent candlestand in memory of her husband Walter Trotter Barton. Walter senior was born at Chilton, Co. Durham, on 8th October 1937. His mother died when he was 10 years old and he was brought up by his father, a coal miner, and his two sisters. He was a choir boy for a number of years, and made a bookcase which stands in Chilton Church. After leaving school he went to Bishop Auckland Technical College and served his apprenticeship in joinery. He was very proud to have put the bell in the tower when Newton Aycliffe New Town was being built.

Walter married Rita and had two boys, Walter and Paul. He went into the RAF to do his National Service and then went to Huddersfield Teacher Training College. He secured a post to lecture in building at Hartlepool College of Further Education, so the family moved to Seaton Carew. He sometimes did jobs for Holy Trinity and helped at the Scouts group when the boys were young. Walter retired at the age of 55 and died three years later aged 58. He was a quiet man and very proud of his family.

Sylvia Lupton

The porch on the south side of the chancel contains a window installed in memory of a much-loved member of the church, Sylvia Lupton. Appropriately for a church with the name Holy Trinity, this is a window with three panes.

Born in Kent, Sylvia lived most of her married life in Seaton Carew. After leaving High School, she spent some time working in Germany as a children's nanny. When first married, she worked for a while for Casper Edgar's travel

Sylvia Lupton memorial window

agency. She and her husband Ken brought up two sons, Martin and Simon and on her sister's death made a home for her niece Karen. They are all married now with families of their own.

Sylvia was an active member of the church, being a member of the now defunct Young Wives' Club; she ran a playgroup and was a church school governor. During the interregnum before Father Paul's arrival, as a member of the Parochial Church Council, she helped with the keeping of the electoral roll. Sylvia died in November 2008 and is much missed by current members of the congregation.

Empire Star memorial

One of the mysteries among the furniture in Holy Trinity is the anonymous donation of an oak display case with a glass top, which holds the Book of Remembrance. It bears the inscription:

To the Glory of God a thank offering
For a great deliverance
SS Empire Star
12th February 1942

The Empire Star was one of the Blue Star Line ships, launched from the Harland & Wolff yard at Belfast under Captain Capon. She became involved in the Second World War when in January 1942 she was sent to join a convoy sailing to Singapore, where the Japanese were mounting an attack. She came to the rescue of a reinforcement troop ship, the Empress of Asia, when it was sunk.

On 11th February 1942, Captain Capon received orders to help with the evacuation of women, children, and selected air force personnel and military nursing staff chosen to escape from Singapore. Things were made worse by army deserters, many from Australia, forcing their way on board.

Empire Star

The Empire Star had to navigate through minefields and was then subjected to an air attack by Japanese dive bombers which lasted for four hours. She suffered three direct hits, which killed 12 of the military personnel on board and injured a further 17, two of whom died later. Despite further attacks, the captain managed to steer the ship to safety with some skill, receiving the CBE for his services, although he attributed the escape to Providence.

Official figures stated 2209 people were on board, but the captain estimated she was carrying around 2,400; the following photograph indicates how crowded the decks were.

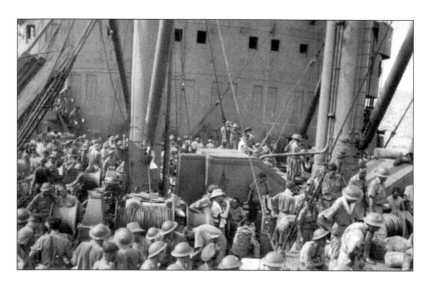

Empire Star deck

The military personnel and civilian evacuees were taken to Batavia (now named Jakarta, in Indonesia), and the Australian nurses and some specially authorised civilian passengers disembarked at Fremantle in Western Australia.

Two local people, Arthur Glendenning and June Markwell, have researched this story and produced a booklet about it, having made several appeals for information, but it has not been possible to identify who placed the memorial in Holy Trinity. It seems likely that the person who gave it was linked to someone who survived the evacuation.

The church inventory deposited in Durham Records Office reveals that this piece of furniture was donated on 12th February 1967:

"A carved Oak Stand to contain the Baptismal Roll – a Thank offering from a parishioner who desires to remain anonymous".

It seems that this is destined to remain a secret.

CHAPTER 19 – REFLECTIONS

The idea for this book came from a meeting of the Restoration Appeal Committee. A suggestion was made that it would be interesting to put on an exhibition of items relating to the church history, and hold a social evening to launch it, as a fund raising effort. It was thought that with a little research, an interesting display could be put together using documents from the vestry trunk and items donated by parishioners.

Somehow, this developed into a proposal for a book, to develop the themes from the previous "Trinity 2000" publication, written to celebrate the Millennium, and to find out more details about the vicars and families who have helped to develop the church into what it is today. When I volunteered to write it, little did I know how much work it would involve, or how absorbed I would become in piecing together the story and trying to solve its mysteries. It soon became evident that there was a vast range of information about Holy Trinity and Seaton Carew, but that it was spread far and wide, begging to be brought together.

Essentially, as I have said from the beginning, this is a story about people – their everyday lives, interesting events and their relationship with the parish church. The villagers lived out their faith through their interactions with each other, building a community that stuck together through good times and bad, and always being ready to lend a helping hand to those who needed support. They may have proved stubborn at times, especially when those in authority tried to ride roughshod over their wishes. But they showed great humanity, especially in responding to others who were overpowered by the sea, whether in active rescue by manning the lifeboats, giving shelter and clean clothes to shipwrecked sailors, or in attending funerals and giving wreaths for those who had no-one else to grieve for them.

The overriding impression from all the information that has been gathered is of a real community spirit. Life could be difficult; there are many infants buried in Holy Trinity's churchyard, large families would have been crowded into quite small homes, and some of the jobs would have been very hard work, often dependent on the weather and the tides. But this was a community that also had an active social life, with many clubs and societies, often based around the church. This sense of joyfulness and fellowship has lasted well throughout Holy Trinity's history, and is still alive today.

This community spirit has also been in evidence as I did the research for this book. Members of today's congregation have assisted with information about their families, or have contributed towards the publishing and printing costs so that we could maximise the proceeds going towards the Restoration Appeal. This has been much appreciated.

Archivists, museum staff and librarians encountered during my research have without exception provided excellent advice, guidance and support. All have responded positively to requests to waive fees for reproducing images and information, when informed of the fund raising purpose of the work.

The truly unexpected experience, however, has been the willingness of complete strangers to support my quest for accurate information, enabling the whole story to be told. I have had some wonderful results from simply sending speculative emails and engaging in exchanges with others. The acknowledgements page shows the extent of the help I have had from willing contributors, which has added richness to the story.

Tracing the development of this parish has also demonstrated how much has changed, yet the core of life in Seaton Carew has stayed the same. When Holy Trinity was built, there were only around 300 residents living in Seaton Carew; it now serves over 6,000. Life is lived at a much faster pace, but the fundamental needs of people have not changed substantially: food and drink, warmth, shelter, relationships, and a core belief which sustains them through life's ups and downs and allows them to celebrate God's creation. We still get visitors and a fine sunny day brings a great influx of people to enjoy the beach and the sea, just as it did in the 1830s when the church was established. Of course some of the other attractions of today are very different.

We have also seen a glimpse of the families who were central to the life of the village. Some members of the community were leaders of industry or made their mark in particular professions such as law, and others had humble occupations. But worship brings all sections of society together, and a church needs everyone to share the work. This study of Holy Trinity and its people shows us the varied contributions that have been made over the years by parishioners young and old, rich and poor, PCC officers and backroom volunteers alike. The windows, furniture and plaques in church are an indication of material contributions, but the intangible elements are built into the very atmosphere of the church: the prayers of the faithful, the unseen work of the cleaners, those who visit the sick, manage the money, plan the social events, and support the vicar in many ways. Thank you to all who do these things and more.

Time spent at church encourages us to slow down, spend some time in silence and prayer, and think about others. I hope that this book will encourage those who visit Holy Trinity to look around at the windows, furniture and memorial tablets, and appreciate the souls of the past who wanted to make their mark in the place where they had worshipped God and celebrated their lives. But let us also give a thought to all who have played a part in the history of Holy Trinity. Thanks be to God for this community.

BIBLIOGRAPHY

TS Turner: History of Aldborough & Boroughbridge

Michelle Guinness: The Guinness Spirit: Brewers, Bankers, Ministers and Missionaries

William Tate: A Description of these highly noted watering places in the County of Durham, Hartlepool & Seaton Carew 1816

Royal Geographical Society: factsheet on the life of Isabella Bird

Anna M Stoddart: The Life of Isabella Bird (Mrs Bishop) 1906

Maureen Anderson: Bygone Seaton Carew an Illustrated History

J H Betty: Church and Parish – A Guide for Local Historians

Mary Tiffen: Friends of Sir Robert Hart – Three Generations of Carrall Women in China

Church records deposited at County Durham Records Office

Diocesan records deposited at Durham University Library, Palace Green

ACKNOWLEDGEMENTS

I have been very fortunate in finding generous people from far and wide, who have been willing to help me in my research and to allow the use of material for this book. Others have helped with the proof reading and given advice on the style. I am indebted to everyone who has helped.

Barbara Mowbray: for permission to use her late husband Derek Hornby's unpublished work, "A Seaton Carew Miscellany"

The Bowes Museum: for permission to use a selection of 8 photographs from the collection by Rev James Pattison

The Trustees of Lambeth Palace Library: for permission to use images from their collection of church building plans and drawings: ICBS 01325 Folios 26 ff.

Hartlepool Reference Library, especially Diane Marlborough

County Durham Record Office

North Yorkshire Record Office

Northumberland Archives Service

Hartlepool Council Museums Service: Mark Simmonds, Charlotte Taylor and Daniel Francis

Hartlepool Council and Carlton Outdoor Centre: for permission to use information on William Wilson Clark from the Carlton Centre website.

Chris Cordner of the Hartlepool Mail: for publicity and assisting in finding information on some of the families

Canadian Archives Service: for information on Revd. C B R Hunter

John Knopp, Snape Local History Group: for information on Charles Tilly

Rob Love: for Lawson family information

Linda Dooks, Boroughbridge Historical Society: for Lawson family information

Barb Angell, Angell Productions: for information on the Empire Star including the photograph of the deck of the ship

Nelson: for information on the Empire Star

Mark Fawcus: for permission to use extracts from his Fawcus family history

Mary Tiffen: for permission to use information from her book on Frances Fawcus' (Carrall) time in China, and transcripts of letters by Anna Maria and Robert Fawcus.

Kathleen Brooks: for information about Ada Charlton, parlour maid with the Thomlinson family.

Gillian Smith: for information on Ralph Thompson Walker

Neil Moat of Newcastle University: for information on the stained glass windows.

John J Tunesi of Liongam, Honorary Secretary, The Heraldry Society: for information on the coats of arms in the Wray window.

Lindsey Hutchinson: for photographs of Thomas Williams and family.

Michael Potts: for information about the clock installed in 1920.

Jill Walters of Christ Church on the Stray, Harrogate: for photographs and information about Revd. Arthur Guinness' tomb and memorial

Pam Smith of Harrogate Family History Society: for assistance in tracing information about Revd. Arthur Guinness and Harrogate

Bill and Mary Worley: for information on the period of Bill's incumbency.

Fellow church members, Edna Holmes, Kath Ness, Adrienne Peterson, Bob Bulmer, Brian Lightfoot, and Diane Barton: for information on the memorials given by their families and friends.

Cheryl Burton: for information and photographs of the Burton family.

Father Paul Allinson: for his encouragement, interest, and patience as I took photographs of the church and talked about little else while doing the research and writing.

Maureen Anderson, local historian and published writer, for information on the lifeboats, letters to Revd. Lawson, proof-reading help and advice.

Carol Cliffe, Father Paul, Patricia Watson and my husband Cliff Cordiner for proof reading and advice.

For donations towards the publishing and printing costs:
Adams Conservatories, Diane Barton, Kath Ness, Mary Tiffen, Terry Lewis, Adrienne Peterson.